Light & Healthy
Mediterranean
Cooking

LIGHT & HEALTHY

MEDITERRANEAN
COOKING

JUDITH WILLS

PHOTOGRAPHY BY
DEBBIE PATTERSON

HPBooks
a division of
PRICE STERN SLOAN
Los Angeles

Throughout the book, recipes are for four people unless
otherwise stated.

Text copyright © Judith Wills 1992
Design and layout copyright © Conran Octopus Limited 1992
Photographs © Debbie Patterson

Published by HP Books
a division of Price Stern Sloan, Inc.
11150 Olympic Boulevard
Suite 650
Los Angeles, California 90064

First published in the UK in 1992 by
Conran Octopus Limited
37 Shelton Street
London WC2H 9HN

Printed in Singapore
10 9 8 7 6 5 4 3 2 1

NOTICE: The information in this book is true and complete to the best of our knowledge. All
recommendations are made without any guarantees on the part of the author or Price Stern Sloan. The author
and publisher disclaim all liability in connection with the use of this information.

This book is printed on acid-free paper.

CONTENTS

FOOD FOR THOUGHT

In this first chapter we look at the way Western man's diet has changed over the centuries and at the strong evidence which points to why today's Western diet is so bad for our health, while the simple diet traditional in Mediterranean countries is the ideal way for us all to eat for many reasons.

For most of the existence of the human species—around 50,000 years—we have lived on a diet consisting largely of unrefined plant foods, such as leaves, seeds, nuts and fruits, supplemented by a little meat or fish when it was successfully hunted. Farmed grains were added to the diet after the first agricultural revolution about 10,000 years ago.

Anthropologists estimate that throughout all of that time, the total fat content of the human diet was no more than about 20%.

A mere 200 years ago, at the start of the Industrial Revolution, the diet of people in the new urban areas of industrial concentration began to change. The resulting changes since have been so drastic that in North America and Western Europe, our diet now consists of around 40% fat, and our consumption of unrefined plant foods has been halved. Instead, "simple carbohydrates" as sugars—virtually unknown to us 200 years ago—now form about 20% of our everyday diet.

Faced with the evidence of such major dietary change in such a relatively very tiny time span, it is easy to see how the modern Western diet could be a major cause of modern Western ills. Heart diseases, strokes and cancer between them now account for over 70% of all deaths in the USA and industrialized Northern Europe.

The problem of having too much to eat has rapidly overtaken the problem of finding enough to eat. Obesity and related problems, such as mid-life diabetes, are now serious epidemics, whereas diseases related to malnutrition, like scurvy and rickets for example, have all but disappeared.

Interestingly, however, the people of the less industrialized areas of the Mediterranean have not succumbed to the sort of high-fat, highly refined diet so prevalent in other areas. These "Mediterraneans" eat a diet which contains a balance of nutrients very similar to that of our ancestors. Their low rates of heart disease and cancer and

OPPOSITE: Breakfast of fresh fruit, fruit juice, crusty bread and Greek-Style Yogurt (page 124)

their longer life expectancy are surely the proof that a prudent diet is the best life insurance we can buy.

Many worldwide cross-cultural studies and an increasing amount of scientific evidence can leave us in little doubt, as we head to the twenty-first century, that what we eat affects our health. If we eat unwisely, we are putting ourselves at unnecessary risk; if we eat wisely we can actually protect ourselves and increase our chances of living longer and healthier lives.

The good news is that, through decades of research into the specific causes of disease, it is now possible for us to be sure of what really constitutes a "healthy diet." This is true both in terms of the amounts of the different food groups we should eat, what we should cut down on for example, and in terms of particular individual foods that can offer us real "health protection"–in other words, foods we should eat more of. The traditional diet of the people who live in the countries bordering the Mediterranean comes closer than any other modern diet to matching this dietary ideal.

DIET & DISORDER

Before looking at the Mediterranean diet in detail, let us examine more closely the current North American diet and its links with the "diseases of affluence," as some now call heart disease, cancer, diabetes, obesity and other disorders.

FATS

The link between a diet high in fat, particularly saturated fat, and increased risk of heart disease, strokes and some forms of cancer is now definitely proven by medical research fundings.

There are three types of fat in our diet:
SATURATED FAT is found mainly in animal products and it is that type of fat which tends to be solid at room temperature. Butter, lard, suet and the fat you see on cuts of meat are all high in saturates. The fat in dairy foods is high in saturates too, as are many margarines. However, the only plant to contain a lot of saturated fat is the coconut.
POLYUNSATURATED FAT is usually found in vegetable oils which are mostly liquid at normal room

NUTRIENTS	1 WHAT WE EAT NOW	2 WHAT WE SHOULD EAT*	
	PERCENTAGE OF DAILY FOOD CALORIE INTAKE	PERCENTAGE OF DAILY FOOD CALORIE INTAKE	
		LOWER LIMIT	UPPER LIMIT
TOTAL FATS	42%	15%	30%
BROKEN DOWN AS:			
SATURATED FATS	27%	NO LOWER LIMIT	10%
POLYUNSATURATED	7%	3%	7%
MONOUNSATURATED	8%	To make up the difference between combined total of saturated and polyunsaturated fats and total fat intake, i.e. between 12% and 13%	
PROTEIN	15–20%	10%	15%
TOTAL CARBOHYDRATES	40–45%	55%	75%
BROKEN DOWN AS:			
SIMPLE CARBOHYDRATES (SUGARS)	20%	0%	10%
COMPLEX CARBOHYDRATES	20–25%	50%	70%
FIBER	20 g	27 g	40 g
SALT	12 g	NOT DETERMINED	6 g

All figures are approximate and average.
* As outlined in "Diet, Nutrition and the Prevention of Chronic Diseases"
(World Health Organization, 1990)

temperature. Oils high in polyunsaturates are corn oil, sunflower oil and safflower oil. Polyunsaturated margarines are made from these oils. Oily fish, such as mackerel, sardines and herring, are also high in polyunsaturates.

MONOUNSATURATED FAT is contained in the highest amounts in olive oil, peanut oil and canola oil.

No one source of fat is 100% saturated, polyunsaturated or monounsaturated. For instance, red meat contains poly- and mono- as well as saturated fat, and just over half the fat in corn oil is polyunsaturated.

Unfortunately, the main source of fat in our diets now is not natural basic foods, such as a slice of roast beef or a spoonful of oil, but the high amount of convenience, packaged foods that we consume. Cakes, pastries, cookies, chocolates, food mixes, packaged desserts and French fries are some of the most obvious items on an endless list of the foods that many of us now regard as normal eating and which are providing us with our huge fat intake without us being really aware of it.

By the 1950s, coronary heart disease (CHD) had become the single major cause of death in the USA and Britain. The relationship between diet and CHD was most famously supported by the Seven Countries Study published in 1980, when it was discovered that high levels of saturated fat intake and blood cholesterol in some countries almost exactly matched those with the highest levels of death from CHD.

Saturated fat in the diet raises blood cholesterol levels which leads to narrowing of the arteries so that the blood literally has difficulty in circulating around the body. The cholesterol also forms into clots which cause strokes and heart attacks. Saturated fats contribute to this effect by stimulating the production of low-density lipoproteins which encourage the depositing of cholesterol.

A diet rich in cholesterol–foods such as eggs, liver and some shellfish–also raises blood cholesterol. However, for the average person, the real problem is saturated fat.

In the Seven Countries Study, Japan had the lowest saturated fat intake at 3% and blood cholesterol was low at 166, while in Finland, saturated fat intake was 22% and blood cholesterol high at 271. CHD deaths over the 15-year period of the study were 144 per 10,000 in Japan–but an alarming 1,202 per 10,000 in Finland!

This study was just one of many international studies to produce results clearly linking saturated fat and high blood cholesterol with CHD.

Diets high in the other types of fat do not produce a similar link. The Eskimos, who eat a diet very high in polyunsaturated fish oils, have a low rate of CHD. The same is true of the peoples of the poorer areas of the Mediterranean, such as Greece and Southern Italy, who eat a diet reasonably high in fat in the form of olive oil, yet have CHD death rates around *half* that of the USA and Britain.

A diet high in saturated fat is also linked with increased risk of some forms of cancer, particularly colon cancer, prostate cancer and breast cancer. According to the World Health Organization, other diseases and conditions that are made worse by eating the typical affluent Western diet include: diabetes, obesity, diverticulitis, gallstones, hemorrhoids, constipation, and arthritis.

PROTEIN

In the late '50s, '60s and '70s, most people's main nutritional worry was whether or not they were getting enough protein in their diet. A meal wasn't regarded as a proper meal unless it contained a large visible portion of an animal protein, such as meat, eggs, fish or poultry.

In fact, we now know that a diet containing as little as 10% protein is adequate and that eating more than about 15% is totally unnecessary. Also, the source of protein doesn't need to be animal. There was much talk in these same decades about high quality and low quality protein. Although it was known that many plant foods contain good amounts of protein, they were considered inferior to animal sources. We now know that plant sources, such as beans and lentils, are as important as the protein in a slab of beef.

In the USA especially, many people also tend to get their protein from convenience foods and/or fatty cuts of meat which also contain high proportions of fat, for example fried meat, hamburgers, hot dogs, and so on.

9

CARBOHYDRATES

The typical diet in the USA and Britain, high in fat and protein, is correspondingly relatively low in carbohydrates–i.e. the foods of plant origin, such as cereals, legumes, seeds, fruit and vegetables. Much of the carbohydrate that we do eat is also refined carbohydrate–sugary products which contain little fiber and, often to make matters worse, a great deal of fat.

As Table 1 (page 8) shows, virtually half of all the carbohydrate we eat is in the form of sugar, i.e. empty calories containing no nutrients at all: no vitamins or minerals, no protein, no fiber–just calories! We each eat on average about 2 pounds of sugar every week, or about 4-1/2 ounces (more than 22 teaspoonfuls) every day! Half of this is bought in packages for use at home; the other half is eaten as candy, cakes, cookies, chocolates, and in canned and other commercially processed foods.

If we are to eat as the WHO recommends in Table 2 (page 8), there is, however, room for only 5% of our daily calories to be in the form of sugar. (If you are eating up to 30% of calories as fat, 15% as protein and 50% minimum as complex, ie unrefined, carbohydrates, that adds up to 95%.) Five percent of the average daily diet of 2,000 calories equals 100 calories–or about 1 ounce of sugar a day, which is only about 5 teaspoonfuls.

The real problem with a diet that relies a lot on convenience and packaged foods is that it is very hard to know exactly how much sugar you *are* eating. However, a diet high in natural unprocessed foods means it is a simple task to limit your added sugar intake. You can then happily add a little sugar or honey to your breakfast yogurt, knowing that you are well within the 5% limit.

FIBER

The typical Western high-fat, high-protein, low-carbohydrate diet also contains too little fiber. The term fiber covers several different types of non-digestible substances found in our diet and present only in plant foods. There is no fiber in animal products and none in fat. A diet low in fiber is linked with an increased risk of colon cancer, diabetes mellitus and diverticulitis plus a wide-range of other digestive disorders.

SALT

As a diet high in salt is linked with high blood pressure and an increased likelihood of high blood pressure and heart disease later in life, the WHO recommends an upper limit of 6 grams a day–about half the intake of many of us at the moment.

Of the salt we eat, about one-third is present in foods naturally; another third is added in cooking and at the table; and the final third is consumed in commercially prepared foods, such as potato chips, cereals, canned vegetables, canned meats, pickles and in take-out and convenience meals.

It is therefore quite easy to see that if we switch to a diet which eliminates most refined convenience foods and if we stop adding salt indiscriminately at the table, we can easily achieve the 6-gram target and still use a little salt in cooking.

TOWARD A HEALTHIER DIET

If we are to cut down on fats, especially saturated fats, and on sugar, and if we are to eat no more protein than we do at present, how are we then to make up the shortfall in calories that this will present–assuming, of course, that we don't want to lose weight! The answer is simply more complex carbohydrates: more grains, such as bread, breakfast cereals, rice, pasta, etc; more legumes, such as beans, peas, lentils; more root vegetables, like potatoes, sweet potatoes and beets; more nuts and seeds; and more fresh fruit and other vegetables.

At present, as Table 1 shows, these foods form no more than 25% of our diet, whereas, as Table 2 shows, the WHO recommends they should constitute at least 50%. Not only do these complex carbohydrates have *no negative effects*–there are no links between them and diseases or ills of any kind–they also have plenty of positive effects. Not only do they provide quantities of fiber for bowel regularity, and have a high content of the various vitamins and minerals we need for good health, but we also now know they offer real, *positive*, protective benefits. These benefits will be discussed in more detail in the next chapter.

The question of complex carbohydrates brings us back to the diet of the Mediterraneans–a diet that relies first on carbohydrates and only to a very small extent on animal products.

Though the Mediterranean countries vary in their preferred foods and styles of cooking—for instance, Italy is the home of pasta and salads, while Moroccans eat more grains, spices and dried fruits—the overall balance of nutrients works out remarkably similarly in all the Mediterranean countries. This balance tallies almost perfectly with the WHO ideals as set out in Table 2.

Some of the Mediterranean peoples do, of course, love their rich desserts and pastries. Traditionally, however, these have been eaten only rarely. They are usually reserved for feast days and celebrations, and are certainly not eaten on a regular daily basis.

Let us examine some of the differences between the daily diet of an average American and that of a Mediterranean person.

BREAKFAST

A cooked breakfast is still a strong feature. Although fried or scrambled eggs, bacon, sausages, hashed brown potatoes, pancakes, waffles, and so on are not now eaten as regularly as they once were, they are still a normal element of brunch on the weekend. Even on a day without a cooked breakfast the average American will have thickly buttered toast and will put whole milk on his cereal or in his coffee.

The Mediterranean breakfast rarely involves anything cooked. It is a high-complex-carbohydrate affair—crusty bread, some fruit preserves (butter is rarely used) and some fresh fruit and/or fruit juice is typical throughout the area. There may sometimes also be yogurt—a low-fat source of easily digested protein. In current nutritional terms, the Mediterranean breakfast is a perfect start to the day.

LUNCH

If the American is eating at home, he or she may well make up for the lack of a cooked breakfast with a hearty meal at lunchtime instead. Alternatively, a can of soup may be opened or an omelette made. If trying to be good and lose weight, he or she will perhaps have a portion of chicken with a small side salad consisting of a few lettuce leaves plus a little thinly sliced cucumber and tomato. To this he or she will probably add some mayonnaise, not realizing that it is a very high-fat high-calorie food.

If eating in the office or on the run, he or she will buy a sandwich (often of white bread) filled with high-fat cheese or meat—or have a hamburger. There may also be a chocolate bar or a slice of cake to follow.

The Mediterranean lunch snack is more likely to be homemade soup, usually based on vegetables or legumes, a plate of cooked beans or a grain such as bulgur dressed with a little olive oil, or some fresh sardines with plenty of crusty whole grain bread and a big salad. Alternatively, there may be a selection of stuffed vegetables or dips and spreads to accompany flat bread—and *always* a salad.

MAIN MEAL

When Americans cook for their families, they first work out what meat or poultry, or other protein source, will form the centerpiece of the meal, and then rather casually decide what vegetable will go

11

with it as an after-thought. Potatoes or some white rice will usually feature, but very often any other vegetable is out of a can or package: Canned corn, green beans and green peas are the norm. There is often a fat-laden dessert–apple pie and chocolate cake are currently two of the most popular desserts for adults, and children eat ice-cream and cookies literally by the ton.

When the Mediterraneans sit down to their main meal of the day, it will most probably be based around a grain, and it will often be a vegetarian meal: perhaps tomato sauce added to pasta, or mushrooms added to rice. There will always also be a variety of vegetables or salad, either in the dish or to accompany it, and fresh fruit afterward.

Because of the scarcity of red meat in the poorer areas of the Mediterranean, it was reserved for special occasions, and many people saw lamb, say, only once or twice a year. Instead, poultry and fish are the two main sources of animal protein. Animal foods are also "stretched," i.e. used in small quantities as a part of a carbohydrate-based meal. High protein legumes are mostly used in their stead.

Without even realizing it, the people of the Mediterranean have been following the kind of diet that the WHO now recommends we all adopt.

Ironically, as the development of the European Community and growing industrialization of rural areas of the Mediterranean increase local awareness of how the citizens of Northern Europe and the USA eat–and as fast-food outlets spring up all over –the villagers of the Mediterranean are beginning to adopt the Western diet themselves. Sadly they, too, are seeing an increase in both heart disease and cancer.

However, they have a long way to go to catch up. The average life expectancy of an Italian man is nearly two years longer than that of a Briton. If Italian health care, expenditure, and facilities had .been comparable to that of Britain over the past 50 years or so, I have no doubt that this gap would be even wider.

Celery & Artichoke Salad (page 109); mixed leaf salad; Vegetable Lasagne (page 96); Melon & Strawberry Salad (page 121)

PROTECTION ON A PLATE

Changing to a really healthy diet means not only cutting down on fats and refined foods and eating much more fiber, but also eating certain "protective" foods. Here we look in detail at such foods – from olive oil to legumes, fruits and vegetables – all abundant in the Mediterranean region.

The first stage in establishing a healthy diet is to get the balance of nutrients right, as outlined in the previous chapter.

However, there have also been new and exciting developments in health/diet research in the last decade as a result of work done around the world by scientists investigating the idea that certain foods actually protect our health.

Including such foods–or, perhaps, including more of them–in the diet actually seems to help protect the body from all kinds of diseases and problems. The risks of developing heart disease, high blood pressure, strokes, some forms of cancer, and digestive disorders can now be greatly reduced, it would seem, by these "protective foods."

Interestingly, some foods seem to offer some protection: members of the cabbage family, dark green and bright orange fruits and vegetables, legumes and garlic ...if there is such a thing as a group of superfoods, then perhaps these are they.

It is precisely these foods, and the others discussed in this chapter, that form the basis of the diet of the Mediterraneans. The grains, the legumes, the fruits and vegetables–even the olive oil and wine– which are the staples of the area provide what now appears to be the ultimate healthy diet.

This chapter examines the protective factors in question, all of which can be easily adapted for a Western diet and palate, with all the same benefits– benefits that can work in as short a time as a few months to improve your health, reduce the risk of ill health in the future, and enhance life expectancy.

NOT ALL FATS ARE BAD

In its recommendations on how we should lower our intake of fats to help prevent coronary heart disease and other ills, the World Health Organization suggests that we should cut our intake of saturated fats by at least half–from levels currently at 20% plus (of total energy intake) down to a maximum of 10%.

OPPOSITE: Raisin-Baked Sardines (page 80)

Although a diet high in polyunsaturated fats can lower blood cholesterol, it suggests that we should not increase our intake of these fats from the current maximum intake of 7%. Their logic regarding this appears to be that if our intake of saturated fats is reduced sufficiently, a 7% intake of polyunsaturates will be enough to maintain reduced blood cholesterol levels.

Interestingly, however, the WHO is quite happy for us to increase our intake of monounsaturated fats. It doesn't actually specify a maximum intake but by implication that figure is 13% (total recommended fat intake is 30%, saturates maximum 10%, polyunsaturates maximum 7%, leaving 13% for monounsaturates). Current monounsaturate intake levels are estimated at between 7 and 10%.

Olive oil is the most widely used oil containing a high proportion of monounsaturates, the only other being peanut oil. Olive oil is, of course, the most favored cooking oil in the Mediterranean. Although butter and other fats and oils are used occasionally, it is the native oil of Greece, Italy and Spain, and features at virtually every Mediterranean meal.

Because of their capacity to lower blood cholesterol, the polyunsaturated fats have received the most attention and the most funds for research over the past 15 years or so. However, the monounsaturates are just as interesting. In fact, worldwide, experts are now beginning to realize that they may be even more beneficial to our health.

In every trial conducted with olive oil so far, it has been shown to have an equally strong capacity to lower blood cholesterol. It also appears to have two very important advantages over polyunsaturates in this respect.

Firstly, a diet high in cholesterol-lowering polyunsaturates but very low in other fats has been shown in trials to have an unfortunate tendency to decrease the levels of the good-for-you High-Density Lipoproteins (HDLs) as well as lowering the levels of bad-for-you Low-Density Lipoproteins (LDLs), which encourage the levels of blood cholesterol to rise.

Secondly, a diet high in polyunsaturates also appears to increase the risk of some forms of cancer. Scientists believe that this is probably because polyunsaturates are very vulnerable to free radical attack, according to a report published in the leading British medical publication, *The Lancet*, in 1991. In other words, they are easily oxidized in our bodies and this means that cell mutations which may lead to the beginnings of cancers may be more easily formed. More work is being done on the exact nature and extent of these links.

In trials, monounsaturated oils have been shown to reduce the cholesterol-encouraging LDLs by up to 21%—while not affecting the beneficial HDLs. Also, because of its different molecular structure, monounsaturated oil is not subject to oxidation in the body. In other words, olive oil appears to lower LDLs and blood cholesterol levels *without* any possible harmful side effects. Meanwhile, the Mediterraneans, who eat a diet relatively high in olive oil but low in saturated fat, have heart disease levels about half those of the British.

Olive oil also offers protection in other areas. It is the most easily digested of fats, and taking it regularly has been shown to improve over half of all stomach ulcers, probably by reducing bile acids and stimulating the action of the pancreas.

It is also likely that a regular intake of olive oil may keep you looking, and feeling, younger for longer. Olive oil may protect you from high levels of the free radicals which experts now believe are the major cause of the ageing process in humans. Free radicals and their action will be examined in more detail later in the chapter.

There is one other type of oil that is of particular benefit in protecting us against heart disease. This is the special type of polyunsaturated oil found in fish, especially oily fish such as sardines, mackerel and tuna—the fish of the Mediterranean.

This particular oil contains Omega-3 fatty acids which have remarkable powers to lower LDLs and blood cholesterol, as well as having other benefits on the circulatory system. The Omega-3s have such a powerful effect in this respect that a mere two portions of oily fish a week can offer real protection.

Although fish is not a cheap commodity in the Mediterranean, it is still eaten on a regular basis, especially the more plentiful fish such as sardines and mackerel. It is certainly eaten more frequently than red meat and even poultry. Mediterraneans

PROTECTION ON A PLATE

also eat a lot of canned fish, such as anchovies, sardines and tuna, which still retain the Omega-3s, and no doubt contribute to their well-being.

COMPLEX CARBOHYDRATES

As we saw in the previous chapter, the Mediterranean diet is made up of a high proportion of complex carbohydrates, such as grains, legumes, root vegetables, nuts and seeds, fruits and vegetables. As well as being able to restore the correct fat/protein/carbohydrate balance to our diets, these complex carbohydrates also offer another major benefit in that they contain different types of fiber.

We all know about roughage, the insoluble fiber contained in bran, for instance, which helps to keep our digestive systems functioning well. However, many complex carbohydrate foods also contain another special sort of fiber which is soluble in water. Being water-soluble, this type of fiber doesn't have the same effect on our digestive systems, but it *does* have one very important effect–it lowers blood cholesterol levels.

A few years ago it appeared that oats were the main source of soluble fiber, but it is now known that the legumes–all the dried beans, peas and lentils–are an even richer source and have an even better ability to lower blood cholesterol. Latest research trials have shown that eating small portions of legumes, equivalent to between 1 ounce and 5 ounces per day, lowers blood cholesterol by between 7% and 26%, depending on the individual's starting level.

Also, while the effect of soluble fiber is to lower bad LDLs, the good HDLs stay the same. In other words, soluble fiber has a very similar effect to foods such as olive oil and fish oils in helping to stave off heart disease. The Mediterranean diet has always relied heavily on legumes of all kinds as a source both of carbohydrate and of protein.

In addition, a diet high in complex carbohydrates also offers protection from some cancers. According to the WHO, "Diets high in plant foods …are associated with a lower occurrence of cancers. Although the mechanisms underlying these effects are not fully understood, such diets are usually low in saturated fat and high in starches and fiber."

More research is being done into the benefits of a diet high in complex carbohydrates. Meanwhile it is prudent to aim for a 55% level.

FRUITS & VEGETABLES

Fruits and vegetables are part of the carbohydrate group of foods. They contain simple carbohydrates, such as fructose (fruit sugar) in fruits for instance, and various types of fiber including the soluble fiber pectin. They also contain some starch: either a very little, as in lettuce, or a lot, as in bananas.

At the moment, we eat only about 7 ounces of fruit or vegetables a day, excluding root vegetables, and the WHO would like that at least to double.

This is not only because all fruits and vegetables are a good source of fiber and the vitamins and minerals which we need regularly for good health and as a protection against deficiency diseases. It also appears that certain vitamins and vitamin-like substances contained in many fruits and vegetables offer real protection against heart disease and certain forms of cancer.

The key vitamins are vitamins C and E, and beta-carotene, a provitamin which converts to vitamin A in our bodies. At one time it was thought that this provitamin was simply a way of obtaining vitamin A, but it now appears to have very special properties that already formed vitamin A from other sources simply does not have.

Fruits and vegetables containing most vitamin C per portion are: citrus fruits, especially oranges; peppers of all colors; broccoli; parsley; Brussels sprouts; all leafy green vegetables; strawberries; guava; mango; melon; and tomatoes. All fruits and vegetables contain some vitamin C.

Foods rich in vitamin E are: vegetable oils including olive oil; nuts; seeds; whole grains; leafy green vegetables; and avocados.

Best sources of beta-carotene are: all yellow, orange, and dark green vegetables, such as carrots, sweet potatoes, squashes, spinach, broccoli, watercress, dark lettuce leaves, tomatoes, asparagus, green peas, cabbage and corn; and yellow and orange fruits, such as mangoes, melons, apricots, peaches, nectarines and oranges.

OVERLEAF: a selection of Mediterranean fruits and vegetables

17

As you can see, most of these fruits and vegetables appear time and again in the diet of the Mediterraneans.

What exactly is so special about these three vitamins? They are anti-oxidants and are important in our diets because they appear to scavenge or inactivate the free radicals which are constantly being produced in our bodies and which can damage cells and tissues by oxidation. If the body's level of anti-oxidants is low, free radicals run wild–and trouble can start. The genetic material of cells may be altered, leading to cancerous states.

According to WHO statistics, an increased intake of fruits and vegetables is linked to a decreased rate of colon cancer, rectal cancer, stomach cancer, and cervical cancer. The latest research from a joint study in France and Singapore also indicates a reduced risk of breast cancer.

Low levels of beta-carotene intake, in particular, are linked with a high risk of lung cancer and oral cancers. Many experts also agree that the anti-oxidant vitamins have a large role to play in preventing heart disease because it may be the oxidation of LDLs by free radicals which causes the narrowing of the arteries.

Lastly, the anti-oxidant vitamins may also play a part in reducing the effects of ageing. The Gerontology Research Center in the USA claims a "great deal of experimental evidence" on this, suggesting that people who increase their intake of the anti-oxidants will age more slowly and delay the onset of diseases associated with old age.

To conclude, the WHO says in its report, "Diet, Nutrition and the Prevention of Chronic Diseases":

"A substantial amount of epidemiological and clinical data indicates that a high intake of plant foods and complex carbohydrates is associated with a reduced risk of several chronic diseases, especially coronary heart disease, certain cancers, hypertension (high blood pressure), and diabetes."

GARLIC

Much-loved by the Mediterraneans for centuries and much ignored elsewhere, garlic has for years had a reputation as a "miracle cure" for all kinds of ills. Many of these were thought old wives' tales, but garlic's power as an antiseptic and antifungal agent is medically proven. Now, it would also seem that a clove or two of garlic a day can help us to health in other ways.

Research has now shown that garlic's active ingredient, allicin, helps to prevent blood clots from forming by dilating blood vessels and by reducing the stickiness of blood. Garlic also lowers blood cholesterol levels *and* it also destroys free radicals. Finally, it can reduce high blood pressure.

All in all, if there really is a "miracle" health food, garlic may perhaps be it! Experts believe that one or two cloves a day are enough to offer protection.

Garlic grows wild in the Mediterranean region and is added to very many of the classic dishes of the area–not because the Mediterraneans knew something we didn't know about the bulb, but simply because they liked the taste!

Onions and other members of the garlic and onion family, such as leeks and chives, probably have a similar, but less potent, healthy effect.

WINE

The Mediterraneans drink wine in preference to any other alcoholic drink, because grapes are abundant and wine is easy to make. It tastes good with meals–which is how they prefer to do their drinking!

The British Heart Foundation and many other expert bodies now agree that moderate alcohol consumption may actually be good for your heart and your health. "A concensus is growing for a beneficial effect," said the BHF in 1991.

Although no one disagrees that over-indulgence of any type of alcoholic beverage is *bad* for your health, up to two glasses of wine a day for women and three for men appear to offer some protection against heart disease by lowering the tendency for the blood to clot.

Sixteen different trials have come to the conclusion that moderate alcohol intake is of benefit. Wine is also an aid to digestion when taken with a meal, as it stimulates the hormones involved in the digestive processes, and it is a relaxant.

If, like the Mediterraneans, you enjoy a glass or two of wine with your meal, perhaps it is time to stop feeling guilty.

OPPOSITE: Olive Oil & Garlic Sauce (page 101)

BALANCING YOUR DIET

Now for the practicalities! Let us discover how to turn your new-found nutritional knowledge into a healthy diet which will not only really work for you, but will fit easily into your own existing life-style and which – above all – you and your friends and family will really enjoy.

How do you put all these new nutritional ideas into practice? How do you make them part of a daily diet that will not only keep you healthy and fit, but that you will find attractive and easy to live with?

Be assured that you will not have to spend your life consulting nutrition manuals, or carrying a calculator around with you in the supermarket to make sure that every meal is perfectly balanced. Common sense is the most important tool.

Firstly, I suggest that you make changes gradually. This is partly for your convenience and partly because a digestive system that has been used to a low-fiber, low-fruit and vegetable, high-fat way of eating needs a little time to adjust. In particular I think it is a good idea to build up slowly your intake of legumes, such as peas, beans and lentils.

After a few weeks, the Mediterranean-style of eating will become second nature to you and you will find you are shopping and eating in a healthier way without even thinking about it. Interestingly enough, should you *then* try to revert to the high-fat, low-carbohydrate way of eating, your digestive system would protest even more.

THE ENERGY TRIANGLE

Let us recap on the three sources of energy (calories) in your diet, and how much of each type you should be eating.

PROTEIN is needed to build and repair lean tissue: muscles, organs, nerves and so on. About 15% of our calories should come from protein. In an average diet of 2,000 calories a day, that represents 300 calories, or 3 ounces of pure protein.

CARBOHYDRATE we need to give us energy. *At least* 55% of what we eat should be carbohydrates, but eating more than this won't do you any harm. The starchy carbohydrates, such as bread, potatoes, pasta and rice, are the foods to fill up on when you are hungry, rather than adding extra animal products to your diet.

OPPOSITE: red mullet; sardines; tomatoes and beans

The only carbohydrates to worry about keeping to a minimum in your diet are highly refined carbohydrates, such as sugar and sugary products. Alcohol consumption also needs to be moderate.

By following the recipes and plans in this book you can be assured that your refined carbohydrate intake will be much lower than levels recommended by the World Health Organization.

On a diet of 2,000 calories per day, your carbohydrate intake should be at least 1,100 calories—or 10 ounces of pure carbohydrate.

FATS & OILS form the remainder of your calories. That is, up to 30%, 600 calories or 2-1/2 ounces of fat. This is a maximum and in theory you could get as little as 10% of your daily calories in the form of fat and still stay in perfect health. In practice, however, a little fat makes other foods more palatable and, as fat is present in so many natural foods, it is extremely hard to lower intake to below 10–20%.

Of this fat, a good balance to aim for is a maximum of about 10% saturated fat, and the other 20% will be made up of monounsaturated fats, such as olive oil, and polyunsaturated fats, such as corn oil.

It is also important to realize that few foods contain only one of the three calorie-givers, that is are all protein, or all carbohydrates or all fat. Most foods are a mixture. For instance, meat and cheese are regarded as protein foods, but even lean meat contains around 10% fat and Cheddar cheese 30%.

For this reason it is best to go for the lower-fat sources of protein most of the time. These include: white fish; shellfish; eggs; low-fat cheeses, such as those soft cheeses made from skim milk, and medium-fat soft cheeses such as Feta and Brie. The Italians love Parmesan cheese which *is* a high-fat cheese; grated, however, a little goes a long way. Chicken and rabbit are excellent low-fat meats and *lean* lamb, beef and pork are perfectly acceptable sources of protein, if eaten in moderation.

High-carbohydrate foods often also contain both protein and fat. For instance, potatoes are a high-carbohydrate food (about 90%) and the rest is mostly protein and a trace of fat.

The complex carbohydrates are all reasonable sources of protein. But those highest in protein are legumes of all kinds, which contain around 30%

protein and little or no fat. Nuts are also a source of carbohydrates, protein and fat.

All this means is that you need only consume small amounts of the animal protein foods to stay healthy. Being careful with the animal sources of protein, especially dairy products, will also lower your saturated fat intake.

VARIETY IS THE KEY
Once you have understood the main need for more carbohydrates and less fat in your diet, perhaps the single most important watchword for healthy eating is simply *variety*.

The easiest way to get all the nutrients you need for health, especially all the vitamins and minerals, is to eat a wide variety of different types of food from within both the high-carbohydrate and high-protein groups. That is because foods of a similar protein or carbohydrate content vary enormously as to their content of vital vitamins and minerals.

Let us compare two high-carbohydrate foods: rice and potatoes. Assuming portion sizes containing a similar number of calories, the potato contains more fiber and potassium, while the rice contains more protein, zinc, and some B vitamins.

Now let us look at two common high-protein foods: chicken and white fish. The chicken is a good source of niacin, while the fish contains more vitamin E and folic acid.

There are hundreds more examples of this sort and it is for this reason that no one food is "the best." *Eat a variety of foods for optimum health!*
● Make a high-carbohydrate food the main part of at least two meals each day, and at least some part of the third meal of the day.
● Include fresh fruits and vegetables or salads at *every* meal, or nearly every meal. Be sure to eat as many red, orange, and yellow fruits and vegetables and leafy green vegetables as you can.
● Eat legumes regularly as the main part of a meal, and use a little nuts and/or seeds every day—they can simply be sprinkled on other foods.

THE RECIPES
The recipes in the book all have a nutrition panel so you can check their value at a glance. I will explain this in a little more detail here.

SATURATED FAT is listed as low, medium or high. Low means less than 5% of the total calorie content of that recipe; medium denotes 5–15%, and high is over 15%. However, *no* recipe in this book is truly high in saturated fat or it would not be included. The maximum I have allowed is 20%.

If you choose a recipe with a medium or high saturated fat content, it makes sense to match it with a very low-fat accompaniment. All the complex carbohydrates contain very little fat, as do fresh fruit and leafy vegetables.

PROTEIN content is also listed low, medium or high. Low means under 15% of total calories; medium denotes 15–20% and high over 20%. If you choose a low-protein dish, say *Stuffed Bell Peppers*, for one meal, pick a high-protein dish at another time in the day. Alternatively, combine a low-protein dish, such as *Mushrooms in Garlic Sauce*, with a high-protein dish at the same meal.

CARBOHYDRATE content is also listed low, medium or high. Low means under 50% of total calories; medium denotes 50-60% and high is over 60%. Some people would consider that a meal containing, say, 49% carbohydrate is not low in carbohydrate at all. However, as I am aiming to get your carbohydrate intake up to at least 55% of your total calorie intake, in my terms under 50% is low. You should try to include at least two high-carbohydrate dishes each day.

FIBER content is listed in grams. You should try to eat at least 25 grams of fiber each day, preferably 30 grams. Remember that you will be getting fiber not just from the recipes but also from accompanying bread, vegetables, salads and fruit, etc. The only foods that do not contain fiber are animal products and highly refined foods such as sugar.

CHOLESTEROL content of the recipes is listed for those who have been advised to cut down the cholesterol in their diets by their doctor. For most of us, however, it is more important to watch intake of saturated fat than cholesterol. A maximum of 300 milligrams a day is perfectly acceptable for everyone. Eggs and shellfish, while being low in fat, *are* high in cholesterol, so it is wise not to have more than one egg or shellfish dish in any one day.

VITAMINS & MINERALS are listed where most abundant in each recipe in order of quantity. Virtu-ally all the recipes will also contain traces of many other nutrients, but if a particular vitamin or mineral is listed it means that this recipe is a particularly good source of it. Watch out especially for recipes high in vitamins C, A (including beta-carotene), E, the B group–B1, B2, niacin, B6, B12, and folic acid –and for dishes rich in iron and calcium.

Salt is optional in most recipes and I recommend that you use as little as you find palatable. If you have been used to a diet high in salt, it is worth retraining your tastebuds to accept less, something the Mediterranean diet can help you to do easily as the profusion of herbs, garlic and spices adds flavor without the need for salt.

THE PLANS
If you look through the menu plans which follow you will see the variety theme working well.

The plans in this chapter are constructed to supply around 2,000 calories a day, which is a reasonable figure for most moderately active women. *Men* will probably need extra, which they should get by increasing intake of complex carbohydrates with, perhaps, a little more higher-protein food, such as poultry, low-fat cheeses or fish.

Wherever a plan includes one of the recipes from the book (indicated in italics), it obviously refers to a single portion (one-fourth of the total) and quantities should be adjusted accordingly.

SPECIAL NEEDS
Vegetarians and vegans will find plenty of suitable recipes, especially in the chapters on Appetizers, Soups & Snacks; Suppers & Lunches; Pasta & Grains, and, of course, Salads & Vegetables. I have also devised vegetarian maintenance and low-calorie plans.

Vegetarians should make sure to eat plenty of dishes rich in the B vitamins, protein, iron and calcium to avoid deficiencies from lack of meat. Legumes are the best source of protein for vegans, who eat no animal products at all.

Children will also enjoy the Mediterranean style of diet. They often have quite high calorie needs for their age and height, and they also need plenty of protein and calcium to build bone and muscle. Teenage girls also often need extra iron.

BUSY SINGLES

QUICK AND CONVENIENT EATING FOR PEOPLE ON THEIR OWN AND IN A HURRY.
ABOUT 2,000 CALORIES PER DAY

Extras per day: 2 glasses (8 oz. each) skim milk, 2 glasses (3-1/2 oz. each) wine (optional).

DAY ONE
BREAKFAST
1/2 cup fresh fruit juice of choice
2 slices of bread with a little low-fat
spread and honey or pure fruit spread

LUNCH
Shrimp Salad
Slice of melon or 1/2 banana

EVENING
Tzatziki with a selection of crudités
Rice with Bell Peppers & Pork
1/2 cup *Greek-Style Yogurt*
2 apricots or 1 oz. dried fruit

DAY TWO
BREAKFAST
2 pieces of fresh fruit of choice
1 cup *Greek-Style Yogurt*
3 tbsp. muesli

LUNCH
Tunisian Eggs
2 slices of bread
1/2 cup vanilla ice milk
1 apple or orange

EVENING
6 oz. fish, broiled with lemon juice
and pepper
Puréed Potatoes
Spinach with Oil & Garlic

DAY THREE
BREAKFAST
3 dried dates or apricots
1/2 cup *Greek-Style Yogurt*
1/2 cup fresh fruit juice of choice
1 slice of bread with pure fruit spread

LUNCH
Slice of melon or 1 peach or
nectarine
Pasta Crunch
1 slice of bread

EVENING
1 pork chop, trimmed of all visible
fat and broiled
Chile-Bell Pepper Sauce
Carrot & Potato Purée
Green Beans in Orange Sauce

DAY FOUR
BREAKFAST
1 whole-wheat muffin with low-fat
spread and pure fruit spread
1 cup *Greek-Style Yogurt* with 2 tsp.
honey
1 orange

LUNCH
2 slices of bread with low-fat spread
1-1/2 oz. low-fat Brie cheese
Carrot, Apple & Beet Salad
1 mango

EVENING
Tomato & Mushroom Risotto
Melon & Strawberry Salad

DAY FIVE
BREAKFAST
As Day One

LUNCH
Assortment of crudités and slices of
toast dipped in
Olive Oil & Garlic Sauce
Tuna Pita Pockets
1/2 cup vanilla ice milk

EVENING
Mushrooms in Garlic Sauce
3 oz. (dry weight) pasta shells,
cooked and served with
Ricotta & Eggplant Sauce
Citrus & Honey Dessert

DAY SIX
BREAKFAST
As Day Two

LUNCH
2 large slices of toast with
Hummus
Large tomato and onion salad with
Oil & Vinegar Dressing
1 banana

EVENING
Tzatziki
Souvlakia
Potato Salad
Green Salad

DAY SEVEN
BREAKFAST
As Day Three

LUNCH
Melted Mozzarella & Tomato
3 slices of crusty bread with
low-fat spread
1 orange

EVENING
3 oz. (dry weight) tagliatelle,
cooked and served with
Walnut Sauce
1 nectarine or peach

TÊTE À TÊTE

A ROMANTIC YET SIMPLE PLAN FOR COUPLES.
ABOUT 2,000 CALORIES PER DAY

Extras per day: 2 glasses (8 oz. each) skim milk, 2 glasses (3-1/2 oz. each) wine (optional –
3 glasses allowed for men).

DAY ONE
BREAKFAST
1/2 grapefruit
2 slices of bread or toast with low-fat
spread and honey

LUNCH
Tomato Salad
Baked Zucchini
1 whole-wheat roll
1/2 cup *Greek-Style Yogurt*

EVENING
Red Pepper Soup
Shrimp Skewers
1/3 cup rice, cooked
Sliced cucumber tossed in olive oil
and pepper
Apple & Date Compote

DAY TWO
BREAKFAST
1/2 cup fresh fruit juice of choice
Mixed Fruit Compote
1/2 cup *Greek-Style Yogurt*

LUNCH
Tunisian Eggs
2 thick slices of bread with low-fat
spread
1 banana

EVENING
Fava Beans & Mushrooms with
1 slice of bread
Lamb Pilaf
Green Salad

DAY THREE
BREAKFAST
1 orange
1/4 cup muesli
1/2 cup *Greek-Style Yogurt*

LUNCH
2 slices of toast with
Tapenade
Stuffed Bell Peppers
Green Salad

EVENING
Baked Sea Bass
Swiss Chard with Pine Nuts
1 (8-oz.) baked potato
1 apple

DAY FOUR
BREAKFAST
2 slices of toast with pure fruit
spread
6 dried dates or apricots

LUNCH
Eggplant Purée with a little pita bread
Mussels with Tomato & Basil Sauce
Slice of melon

EVENING
Mushrooms in Garlic Sauce
Pork Tenderloin Marsala
3 oz. (dry weight) noodles, cooked
Green Salad
1 orange

DAY FIVE
BREAKFAST
As Day One

LUNCH
Minestrone Soup with 1/2 portion of
Pesto stirred into it
1 large bread roll
1 banana

EVENING
Crab & Melon Salad
3 oz. (dry weight) pasta of choice,
cooked and served with
Walnut Sauce
Orange & Fennel Salad

DAY SIX
BREAKFAST
As Day Two

LUNCH
Bean Dip with a selection of crudités
"The Priest Fainted"
1 mango or 4 apricots

EVENING
Ricotta-Stuffed Tomatoes
Squid in Red Wine
Green Salad
Melon & Strawberry Salad

DAY SEVEN
BREAKFAST
As Day Three

LUNCH
Salade Niçoise
2 slices of bread
1 apple

EVENING
Asparagus with Lemon Vinaigrette
Lamb in White Wine
1/3 cup rice, cooked
2 apricots or 1 slice of melon

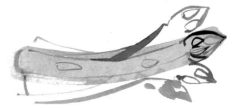

THE FAMILY PLAN

MEALS ALL THE FAMILY WILL ENJOY—BUT WHICH ARE NOT TOO
TIME-CONSUMING FOR THE COOK!
ABOUT 2,000 CALORIES PER DAY

Extras per day: for adults, 2 glasses (8 oz. each) skim milk; for children, 3 glasses (8 oz. each)
low-fat milk.

DAY ONE
BREAKFAST
Mixed Fruit Compote
1/2 cup Greek-Style Yogurt
with 1 tsp. honey

LUNCH
Minestrone Soup
Pissaladina

EVENING
Raisin-Baked Sardines
1 (7-oz.) baked potato
Green Salad
Citrus & Honey Dessert

DAY TWO
BREAKFAST
2 slices of bread with low-fat spread
and pure fruit spread
1/2 cup fresh fruit juice of choice

LUNCH
Hummus with a selection of crudités
Stuffed Eggplant

EVENING
3 oz. (dry weight) spaghetti, cooked
and served with
Tomato Sauce
Apple & Date Compote
1/2 cup vanilla ice milk

DAY THREE
BREAKFAST
1/4 cup muesli with skim milk
5 oz. fresh fruit of choice
1 slice of bread with low-fat spread
and honey

LUNCH
Lamb in Yogurt Sauce
1/2 pita bread
Sliced cucumber

EVENING
Honeyed Chicken
Puréed Potatoes
Swiss Chard with Pine Nuts
1 banana

DAY FOUR
BREAKFAST
1 cup *Greek-Style Yogurt* with
2 tsp. honey
1/2 cup fresh fruit juice of choice
2 oz. dried apricots

LUNCH
Eggplant Purée with a selection of
crudités and toast
Pasta Crunch
1 orange

EVENING
Rabbit Stiphado
5 oz. carrots
1 (8-oz.) baked potato
1/2 cup vanilla ice milk

DAY FIVE
BREAKFAST
As Day One

LUNCH
Lentil Soup
2 or 3 slices of French bread
1 peach

EVENING
Vegetable Lasagne
Green Salad
Baked Pears
1/2 cup *Greek-Style Yogurt*

DAY SIX
BREAKFAST
As Day Three

LUNCH
Bean Salad
Tuna Pita Pockets
1 apple

EVENING
Carrot & Potato Purée with a
selection of crudités
Tomato & Mushroom Risotto
1/2 portion *Mixed Fruit Compote*

DAY SEVEN
BREAKFAST
As Day Four

LUNCH
Tuscan Bean Casserole
2 slices of bread
Tomato Salad

EVENING
Roast Lamb or
Lamb & Apricot Casserole
1 (8-oz.) baked potato
Green Beans in Orange Sauce

GOURMET DELIGHTS

FOR THOSE WHO ENTERTAIN A GREAT DEAL, OR SIMPLY ENJOY A TOUCH OF LUXURY
AND LOVE TO COOK.
ABOUT 2,000 CALORIES PER DAY

Extras per day: 2 glasses (8 oz. each) skim milk, 3 glasses (3-1/2 oz. each) wine or champagne.

DAY ONE
BREAKFAST
1/2 grapefruit
1/2 cup *Greek-Style Yogurt*
with 1 cup strawberries and
3 tbsp. muesli

LUNCH
Roasted Yellow Pepper Dip with a
selection of crudités
Crab & Melon Salad
2 slices of French bread with low-fat
spread

EVENING
Ricotta-Stuffed Tomatoes
2 slices of French bread dipped in
Olive Oil & Garlic Sauce
Chicken with 30 Cloves of Garlic
Puréed Pumpkin
Green Beans in Orange Sauce

DAY TWO
BREAKFAST
Mixed Fruit Compote
1 slice of bread with honey

LUNCH
Mixed Mediterranean Platter
1 mango with
1/2 cup *Greek-Style Yogurt*

EVENING
Swordfish Steaks with Almond Sauce
Spinach with Garlic & Oil
1 medium boiled potato
Peaches in Wine

DAY THREE
BREAKFAST
1 cup *Greek-Style Yogurt*
1 banana
1 orange
1 tsp. honey

LUNCH
Red Pepper Soup
Shrimp Salad

EVENING
Eggplant Purée with a selection of
crudités
Tzatziki
Souvlakia
Pita bread
Tomato Salad

DAY FOUR
BREAKFAST
3/4 cup muesli with skim milk and
1/2 cup fresh fruit of choice

LUNCH
Asparagus with Lemon Vinaigrette
Scallops with Mushrooms
2 slices of French bread

EVENING
Pork with Oranges
5 oz. broccoli
Carrot & Potato Purée
Banana and Strawberry Sorbets

DAY FIVE
BREAKFAST
As Day One

LUNCH
*Three-Nut Salad with Apricots &
Raisins*
2 slices of bread
Slice of melon with chopped mint

EVENING
Mushrooms in Garlic Sauce
Paella
Green Salad

DAY SIX
BREAKFAST
As Day Two

LUNCH
Avocado with Mâche
2 slices of bread
1 banana
1 fresh apricot

EVENING
Celery & Artichoke Salad
Spicy Monkfish Kabobs
1/3 cup rice, cooked with a little
saffron
Citrus & Honey Dessert

DAY SEVEN
BREAKFAST
As Day Three

LUNCH
Seafood Salad with Citrus Dressing
3 slices of French bread

EVENING
Couscous
Melon & Strawberry Salad

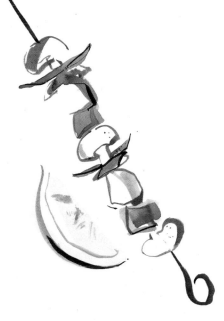

LACTO-OVO-VEGETARIAN PLAN

A HEALTHY PLAN FOR THOSE WHO DON'T EAT MEAT, FISH OR POULTRY.
ABOUT 2,000 CALORIES PER DAY

Extras per day: 2 glasses (8 oz. each) skim milk, 2 glasses (3-1/2 oz. each) wine
(optional).

DAY ONE
BREAKFAST
1 cup *Greek-Style Yogurt* with
2 tsp. honey
Slice of melon
1 orange

LUNCH
Tuscan Bean Casserole
2 slices of bread
1/2 cup vanilla ice milk

EVENING
Eggplant Purée with a selection of
crudités
3 oz. (dry weight) tagliatelle or pasta
spirals, cooked and served with
Walnut Sauce
Baked Pears

DAY TWO
BREAKFAST
Mixed Fruit Compote
1/2 cup fresh fruit juice of choice
1/2 cup *Greek-Style Yogurt*

LUNCH
Feta Pita Pockets
Green Salad

EVENING
Hummus with a selection of crudités
Tunisian Eggs
2 slices of French bread
1 apple
1/2 cup *Greek-Style Yogurt*

DAY THREE
BREAKFAST
2 slices of bread with low-fat spread
and pure fruit spread
1 banana
1/2 cup fresh fruit juice of choice

LUNCH
*Fava Bean & Pasta Salad in Orange
Sauce*
Green Salad
6 fresh or dried dates

EVENING
Mushrooms in Garlic Sauce
Stuffed Bell Peppers
Mixed Fruit Compote

DAY FOUR
BREAKFAST
1 cup *Greek-Style Yogurt* with
2 tsp. honey
1 cup grapes
1 slice of bread with pure fruit spread

LUNCH
*Three-Nut Salad with Apricots &
Raisins*
1 slice of bread with low-fat spread

EVENING
3 oz. (dry weight) pasta shells,
cooked and served with
Ricotta & Eggplant Sauce
Green Salad
Citrus & Honey Dessert

DAY FIVE
BREAKFAST
As Day One

LUNCH
Red Pepper Soup
2 oz. low-fat Brie cheese with a
selection of crudités and toast

EVENING
Tomato & Mushroom Risotto
1/2 cup vanilla ice milk
Slice of melon or 1 peach

DAY SIX
BREAKFAST
As Day Two

LUNCH
Avocado with Mâche
2 slices of bread
Bean Dip with a selection of crudités

EVENING
Vegetable Lasagne
Green Salad
1 banana
1 orange

DAY SEVEN
BREAKFAST
As Day Three

LUNCH
2 slices of French bread with
Olive Oil & Garlic Sauce
Lentil Soup
2 fresh apricots

EVENING
Fava Beans & Mushrooms
Baked Zucchini
1 orange

LATE PREGNANCY

IN THE FIRST FEW MONTHS OF PREGNANCY YOU HARDLY NEED TO EAT ANY EXTRA
CALORIES. HOWEVER, IN THE LAST FEW MONTHS YOU DO NEED MORE! THIS PLAN
PROVIDES ALL THE NECESSARY CALORIES PLUS EXTRA IRON AND CALCIUM.
ABOUT 2,300 CALORIES PER DAY

Extras per day: 2 glasses (8 oz. each) skim milk; yogurt and low-fat cheese whenever you like.

DAY ONE
BREAKFAST
1/4 cup muesli with skim milk
1 banana
2 slices of bread with low-fat spread
and honey

LUNCH
Feta Pita Pockets
Hummus with a selection of crudités
1 orange

EVENING
Orange & Fennel Salad
6 oz. fish, broiled
1 medium boiled potato
1/2 portion *Mixed Fruit Compote*

DAY TWO
BREAKFAST
1 cup *Greek-Style Yogurt* with
2 tsp. honey
3 tbsp. muesli
6 dried apricots
1/2 cup fresh fruit juice

LUNCH
Pasta Crunch
Large slice of melon

EVENING
Roast Lamb
Potato Salad
Bell Pepper & Tomato Stew
Apple & Date Compote

DAY THREE
BREAKFAST
As Day One

LUNCH
Lentil Soup
3 slices of French bread
1 orange

EVENING
1 (9 oz.) swordfish steak, broiled
Chile-Bell Pepper Sauce
Tabbouleh
Banana & Strawberry Sorbets

DAY FOUR
BREAKFAST
As Day Two

LUNCH
"The Priest Fainted"
1/4 cup cottage cheese
2 slices of bread
Green Salad
2 fresh apricots

EVENING
Chicken with Pine Nuts
1/2 cup rice, cooked
1 cup strawberries with
1/2 cup *Greek-Style Yogurt*

DAY FIVE
BREAKFAST
As Day One

LUNCH
Bean Dip with a selection of crudités
Melted Mozzarella & Tomato
2 slices of French bread

EVENING
Ricotta-Stuffed Tomatoes
2 oz. (dry weight) pasta, cooked and
served with
Lentil Sauce
Green Salad

DAY SIX
BREAKFAST
As Day Two

LUNCH
Minestrone Soup
Stuffed Bell Peppers
2 slices of bread
1 orange

EVENING
Sardinian Seafood Stew
1 medium boiled potato
Green Salad

DAY SEVEN
BREAKFAST
As Day One

LUNCH
Lentil & Tomato Salad
2 slices of bread
1 banana

EVENING
Celery & Artichoke Salad
Lamb Pilaf
Strawberry & Melon Salad

LOSING WEIGHT
WHILE EATING WELL

Excess weight is a very serious problem in most Western countries and is in itself a health risk. In this chapter we look at just why obesity is such a great problem. You will also discover how to diet healthily on a really tasty Mediterranean-style diet – without feeling hungry!

It is estimated that at least one-third of the adult population of the Western nations is trying to lose weight at any given time. There are approximately five million *seriously* overweight people in Britain, and in the USA there are more overweight teenagers and young people than ever before.

In other words, despite the availability of thousands of different diets and diet aids, diet magazines, reduced-caloric foods, and advice from health professionals–and despite the fact that most people do realize that being overweight is a real health hazard –obesity is just as much of a problem as ever.

To understand why this is so I think we have to look at the food industry giants who know that packaged products are the ones that make them most profit, not basic fresh foodstuffs. They also finance the multi-billion dollar food advertising industry which persuades us at every turn to buy convenience foods, to follow food fashion fads and, quite simply, to eat *more*.

The fact is that, although according to government statistics we are eating less fat in its original state–butter, margarine, lard–and less refined sugar, our overall consumption of fat and sugar has *not* gone down. The fact is that the food manufacturers simply help us to eat what we are not eating in our own cooking by adding more to canned and packaged foods and in fast food.

Ironically, the people of the more affluent industrialized areas of the Mediterranean are now abandoning their healthy traditional diet in favor of a more Western diet. Imports of butter, white flour and sugar are actually on the increase in this region. Consequently, the populations of these areas are getting fatter and suffering more ill health as a result. This should be a warning to us–and to them!

EATING TO LOSE WEIGHT
You can, in fact, eat pasta and oil, rice and bread, and many other good things, including honey and

OPPOSITE: Healthy food to enjoy while losing weight

desserts, and still *lose weight*! It is interesting that Americans watching their weight always appear guilty at the thought of tucking into a plate of pasta, or anything with oil on it or in it.

In reality, pasta and most of the rest of the foods of the Mediterranean *are not* fattening. The recipes and foods in this book, wisely used, make a delicious, low-calorie diet with a great variety of menu choices for the easiest-ever weight loss.

One of the reasons for its effectiveness is that we virtually eliminate all those packaged convenience foods that almost always contain hidden calories. Instead, you know exactly what you are eating. Another reason is that the Mediterranean diet does not rely on much added fat or sugar, or on a lot of fatty meat and animal products. So you can easily cope with the calories in the pasta and other carbohydrates and the oil that you will eat. These are the *real* convenience foods–they are not complicated to prepare, they are ready quickly, and, above all, they are healthy!

It is true that olive oil, when compared weight for weight with other foods, is high in calories. However, *you* control the amount you use in recipes and sauces at the table. The taste of olive oil is rich, and you need very little to add superb flavor to any dish. In the Mediterranean, no good chef uses so much olive oil that it is either visible when the dish is served or, with few exceptions, a dominant flavor. Even the high-oil dishes such as *Pesto* and oil-and-vinegar dressing are only intended to coat foods lightly–not to drown them.

Let us compare calorie content in a day's eating in North America and in the Mediterranean. The day's eating on the left is fairly typical of the kind of menu that you will find throughout the USA, however with small portions. It is a diet which contains nearly 40% fat, nearly 20% protein and only just over 40% carbohydrate. Although its calorie content is not excessively high, its high-fat, low-carbohydrate content means that it is most certainly not a healthy style of eating.

The Mediterranean-style diet on the right has less than 30% fat, 15% protein and over 55% carbohydrate and the saturated fat content is less than 10%. If you look carefully at the diet on the right, you will probably agree with me that there appears

NORTH AMERICA		MEDITERRANEAN	
Calories		Calories	
BREAKFAST		BREAKFAST	
1 soft-cooked egg	80	1/2 cup yogurt	67
1-1/2 slices of bread	100	1 tsp. honey	20
1-1/2 tsp. butter	53	1-1/2 slices of bread	100
2 tsp. jam	40	Low-fat spread	20
1/2 cup orange juice	50	2 tsp. pure fruit spread	20
		1/2 cup orange juice	50
LUNCH		LUNCH	
2 slices of bread	140	3 slices of bread	210
1 tbsp. mayonnaise	105	2 oz. Feta cheese	150
1 oz. Cheddar cheese	240	Mixed salad of tomato,	
1 oz. cooked ham	65	bell pepper, onion	40
1 dill pickle	30	1 tbsp. oil and vinegar	
1 tangerine	25	dressing	80
		1 peach	50
EVENING		EVENING	
1 4 oz. hamburger		*Celery & Artichoke*	
or steak, broiled	235	*Salad*	108
6 oz. French fries	420	3 oz. (dry weight) pasta,	
2/3 cup green peas	60	cooked, with	300
1 slice of apple pie	250	*Tomato Sauce*	87
3 tbsp. whipped		1-1/2 tbsp. Parmesan	
cream	150	cheese	20
1 cup whole milk	126	*Melon & Strawberry*	
		Salad	80
		1/2 cup yogurt	67
		1 cup skim milk	70
Total for day	2169	Total for day	1539

to be *more* to eat, and a better variety of food, than in the diet on the left. You would certainly not consider yourself on a low-calorie diet when eating all that wonderful-sounding food, would you?

And yet the day's eating on the right contains 600 calories *less* than the other. It is a diet on which all men–and many women–would lose weight, albeit slowly.

Most men need around 2,700 calories a day, so they'd be cutting calories by 1,000 a day or more, to produce a weekly loss of about 2 pounds. Most women need around 2,100 calories a day, so they would be eating about 600 calories a day less than they need to maintain weight–enough to produce a 1 to 1-1/2 pound loss a week.

However, by making a few more changes to the diet on the right, it is easy to bring its calorie content down even more, to about 1,200 calories, for faster weight loss.

To do this you could easily forgo the low-fat spread at breakfast, have 2 slices of bread and 1-1/2 ounces cheese at lunchtime, have 2 ounces pasta in the evening with a slice of melon rather than the fruit salad, and omit the yogurt. This would save another 300 calories while still leaving you a satisfying diet.

What we are doing to help you lose weight is to reduce the fat content of the diet but keep the carbohydrate content high. It is the carbohydrate foods such as pasta, rice and potatoes that help keep you feeling full, with no dangerous hunger pangs between meals.

To explain this in more detail, here are the percentages of carbohydrate, fat and protein in three different diets.

NORTH AMERICAN DIET
Calories about 2,000
Carbohydrate 45% /900 cal/225 g
Fat 35% /700 cal/77 g
Protein 20% /400 cal/100 g

MEDITERRANEAN DIET
Calories about 2,000
Carbohydrate 55% /1,100 cal/275 g
Fat 30% /600 cal/66 g
Protein 15% /300 cal/75 g

LOW-CALORIE MEDITERRANEAN DIET
Calories about 1,200
Carbohydrate 65% /780 cal/195 g
Fat 20% /240 cal/270 g
Protein 15% /180 cal/45 g

From these figures you may see that the low-calorie Mediterranean diet gives you 87% of the carbohydrate of the North American diet, and over 70% of the carbohydrate of the normal Mediterranean diet. This is why it is a good way to diet: It keeps protein at a safe level of 45 grams (the US recommended daily amount for most women is 44 grams) and the fat content of 20%–about 1 ounce a day–allows you room to indulge in olive oil, a little meat, and so on.

As carbohydrates, weight for weight, contain fewer calories by far than fat (carbohydrate has 4 calories per gram and protein has 4 calories per gram, while fat has 9 calories per gram), if you cut animal fat from your diet it is easy to eat enough and stay slim.

Even more interestingly the latest research trials in the US show that a diet high in complex carbohydrates, such as the Mediterranean diet, speeds up the metabolic rate of your body so that there is a further benefit–you are actually burning up the calories you eat more quickly than if you ate, say, a high-fat diet!

So by following the Mediterranean diet, you can lose weight easily. Moreover, because it is so easy to eat less while feeling full, it is highly unlikely that you will ever put weight back on and need to diet again.

Let me summarize the reasons why a Mediterranean diet is the perfect way to lose weight:
● Meals have real filling power–you never finish a meal feeling hungry.
● Hunger pangs are kept away until the next meal because of the high bulk–plenty of fruit, vegetables, and complex carbohydrates.
● The diet is tasty and therefore tastebuds are always satisfied–ordinary diet food seems worlds away.
● The dishes are colorful and appealing to the eye– a very important factor for dieters.
● Motivation to stay with your diet is high because there is *no deprivation* factor involved.

THE PLANS
The low-calorie plans at the end of this chapter can help everyone to lose weight. I have devised nine different plans so that you may choose whichever one best suits your tastes and your lifestyle. Most supply around 1,200 calories a day, which will achieve a weight loss of about 2 pounds per week for women. Men and teenagers could add extra calories to the diet in the form of extra carbohydrates up to 1,500 a day and still lose weight.

I would not advise you to diet on much fewer calories a day than the levels I have set out. Reducing your food intake too low often results in strong feelings of hunger and deprivation which for most people, sooner or later, end in breaking the diet.

You can swap around the lunch and evening meal if you prefer—and also switch from one plan to another, week after week, to add interest. However, because the plans are nutritionally balanced, it is best not to swap from day to day.

As with the plans in the last chapter, references to recipes from the book (indicated in italics) obviously refer to single portions (one quarter of the total) and quantities should be adjusted accordingly.

HOW MUCH DO YOU NEED TO LOSE?
Decide how much weight you need to lose with the help of the height/weight chart on page 128. If you are near target-weight but are not happy with your shape, it could be that you need to do some regular exercise to tone up your body.

OTHER TIPS TO HELP YOU DIET
● When you are full at a meal, stop eating. If there is, say, a fruit dessert left, save it for a snack later. Eat slowly, and concentrate on enjoying each mouthful of your food.
● Don't skip meals when you are dieting—you will only become too hungry and be inclined to over-eat later. If you eat regularly, your blood sugar levels remain constant and this helps you to feel good.
● Take some regular daily exercise. Walking, swimming, bicycling, and aerobics are all good forms of exercise to help burn off calories. A toning routine will also help to reshape your body and firm you up as you lose weight.

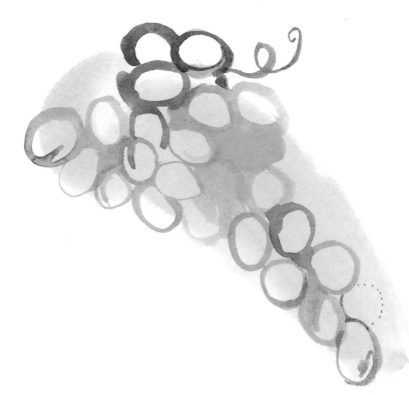

FAST & SIMPLE

QUICK AND EASY-TO-PREPARE MEALS FOR BUSY DIETERS.
ABOUT 1,100 CALORIES PER DAY

Extras per day: 2 glasses (8 oz. each) skim milk.

DAY ONE

BREAKFAST
Mixed Fruit Compote
1/2 cup fresh orange juice

LUNCH
Melted Mozzarella & Tomato
Green Salad
1 peach

EVENING
Souvlakia
Tzatziki
Sliced tomato and onion salad,
garnished with parsley

DAY TWO

BREAKFAST
1/2 cup *Greek-Style Yogurt* with
1 tsp. honey and 3 chopped dried
apricots
1 slice of bread with pure fruit spread

LUNCH
Tuna Pita Pockets
1 orange

EVENING
2 oz. (dry weight) spaghetti, cooked
and served with
Tomato Sauce and 1 tbsp. grated
Parmesan cheese
Green Salad

DAY THREE

BREAKFAST
2 slices of bread with a little low-fat
spread and pure fruit spread
1/2 grapefruit

LUNCH
1 chicken breast half, sprinkled with
rosemary and thyme and broiled
Orange & Fennel Salad

EVENING
Baked Zucchini
Tomato Salad
2 slices of bread

DAY FOUR

BREAKFAST
Fresh fruit platter:
fruit of choice
1/4 cup low-fat cottage cheese

LUNCH
Pasta Crunch
Sliced cucumber and onion salad

EVENING
Spicy Monkfish Kabobs
1/3 cup rice, cooked
Green Salad

DAY FIVE

BREAKFAST
As Day One

LUNCH
Bean Dip with a selection of crudités
1 slice of bread
1 oz. low-fat Brie cheese
1 apple

EVENING
Pork with Oranges
1 cup each cooked carrots and
broccoli
Melon & Strawberry Salad

DAY SIX

BREAKFAST
As Day Two

LUNCH
Crab & Melon Salad
2 slices of bread with a little low-fat
spread

EVENING
3 oz. (dry weight)
fettuccine, cooked and served with
Mushroom Sauce
Green Salad
Citrus & Honey Dessert

DAY SEVEN

BREAKFAST
As Day Three

LUNCH
Feta Pita Pockets
1/2 cup *Greek-Style Yogurt*
1 orange

EVENING
Shrimp Provençal
1/3 cup rice, cooked
Green Salad
Peaches in Wine

THE FAMILY DIET

LOSE WEIGHT WITH MEALS WHICH ALL THE FAMILY WILL ENJOY. THOSE WHO ARE
NOT DIETING CAN EAT MORE BREAD, POTATOES, PASTA OR RICE THAN THE
QUANTITIES GIVEN.
ABOUT 1,200 CALORIES PER DAY

Extras per day: 2 glasses (8 oz. each) skim milk.

DAY ONE
BREAKFAST
1/2 cup fresh fruit juice of choice
1/2 portion *Mixed Fruit Compote*
1/2 cup *Greek-Style Yogurt*

LUNCH
Salade Niçoise
1 cup grapes or strawberries

EVENING
Rabbit Stiphado
1 medium potato, boiled or baked
1 cup green vegetables of choice,
lightly cooked

DAY TWO
BREAKFAST
2 slices of bread with a little low-fat
spread and honey
1 orange

LUNCH
Lentil & Tomato Soup
Lettuce and cucumber

EVENING
Spicy Monkfish Kabobs
1/4 cup rice, cooked

DAY THREE
BREAKFAST
1/4 cup muesli
with 1/2 cup skim milk
1 orange

LUNCH
"The Priest Fainted"
1 slice of bread
1/2 cup vanilla ice milk

EVENING
Lamb & Apricot Casserole
1/4 cup hot cooked rice
Lettuce garnish

DAY FOUR
BREAKFAST
As Day one

LUNCH
Mixed Mediterranean Platter
2 fresh apricots

EVENING
Vegetable Lasagne
Green Salad
Melon & Strawberry Salad

DAY FIVE
BREAKFAST
As Day Two

LUNCH
Minestrone Soup
1-1/2 slices of bread
1 apple

EVENING
9 oz. white fish of choice, broiled
Tomato Sauce
2 small boiled potatoes
Green Beans in Orange Sauce

DAY SIX
BREAKFAST
As Day Three

LUNCH
Feta Pita Pockets

EVENING
3 oz. (dry weight) pasta of
choice, cooked and served with
Mushroom Sauce
Apple & Date Compote

DAY SEVEN
BREAKFAST
As Day One

LUNCH
Baked Zucchini
1-1/2 slices of bread
5 oz. soft fruit of choice with
a little *Greek-Style Yogurt*

EVENING
Rice with Bell Peppers & Pork
Green Salad
1 apple

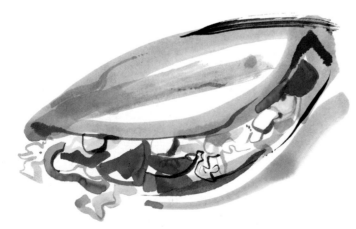

THE ROMANTIC DIET

SERVE VERY SPECIAL MEALS FOR YOU AND YOUR PARTNER - WITHOUT YOUR
OTHER HALF NECESSARILY EVEN KNOWING YOU ARE BOTH DIETING!
ABOUT 1,200 CALORIES PER DAY

Extras per day: 2 glasses (8 oz. each) skim milk, 1 glass (3-1/2 oz.) dry wine. Partners may
add extra rice, potatoes, pasta or bread to each meal if they are not dieting.

DAY ONE
BREAKFAST
1/2 grapefruit or
1/2 cup tomato juice
1/2 cup *Greek-Style Yogurt*
1 slice of bread with a little low-fat
spread and 2 tsp. honey or pure fruit
spread

LUNCH
*Three-Nut Salad with Apricots
& Raisins*

EVENING
*Celery & Artichoke Salad
Mussels with Tomato & Basil Sauce*
1 slice of bread
Peaches in Wine

DAY TWO
BREAKFAST
As Day One

LUNCH
Tapenade with 1–2 slices of toast
Crab & Melon Salad

EVENING
*Honeyed Chicken
Pumpkin Purée*
1 cup lightly cooked broccoli

DAY THREE
BREAKFAST
As Day One

LUNCH
*Fava Bean & Pasta Salad in
Orange Sauce*
1 slice of bread

EVENING
*Squid in Red Wine
Green Salad
Melon & Strawberry Salad*

DAY FOUR
BREAKFAST
As Day One

LUNCH
Melted Mozzarella & Tomato
1 large slice of bread

EVENING
2 oz. (dry weight) pasta of
choice, cooked and served with
*Ricotta & Eggplant Sauce
Green Salad*

DAY FIVE
BREAKFAST
As Day One

LUNCH
Avocado with Mâche
3 fresh apricots

EVENING
*Red Pepper Soup
Lamb in White Wine*
3 tbsp. rice, cooked

DAY SIX
BREAKFAST
As Day One

LUNCH
*Seafood Salad with Citrus
Dressing*
1 slice of bread

EVENING
Pork with Oranges
1-1/2 oz. (dry weight) noodles,
cooked
1 cup green beans, lightly cooked

DAY SEVEN
BREAKFAST
As Day One

LUNCH
Tunisian Eggs
1 large slice of bread
1 cup strawberries

EVENING
Shrimp Provençal
1/3 cup rice, cooked
Green Salad

THE SEMI-VEGETARIAN DIET

A DIETING PLAN FOR ALL THOSE WHO DON'T EAT RED MEAT BUT OCCASIONALLY
ENJOY MEALS WHICH INCLUDE FISH OR POULTRY.
ABOUT 1,200 CALORIES PER DAY

Extras per day: 2 glasses (8 oz. each) skim milk.

DAY ONE
BREAKFAST
1/2 portion *Mixed Fruit Compote*
1/2 cup *Greek-Style Yogurt*

LUNCH
Hummus with 2 slices of toast
Slice of melon or 1 orange

EVENING
Tomato & Mushroom Risotto
Lettuce garnish
1 banana

DAY TWO
BREAKFAST
1/2 grapefruit
3 tbsp. muesli with
1/2 cup skim milk

LUNCH
Tuna Pita Pockets
3 dried apricots

EVENING
Raisin-Baked Sardines
Green Salad
1 apple

DAY THREE
BREAKFAST
1 orange
1 large slice of bread with a little
low-fat spread and 2 tsp. honey

LUNCH
Ratatouille with 1 poached egg
on top
1 large slice of bread
4 fresh or dried dates

EVENING
3 oz. (dry weight)
spaghetti, cooked and served with
Pesto
Lettuce dinner salad

DAY FOUR
BREAKFAST
As Day One

LUNCH
"The Priest Fainted"
1 large slice of bread
1 peach or nectarine

EVENING
Shrimp Skewers
1/3 cup rice,
cooked
Sliced cucumber
Citrus & Honey Dessert

DAY FIVE
BREAKFAST
As Day Two

LUNCH
Tuscan Bean Casserole
1 slice of bread
Lettuce dinner salad

EVENING
Baked Zucchini
Tomato Salad
2 slices of bread
Apple & Date Compote

DAY SIX
BREAKFAST
As Day Three

LUNCH
Salade Niçoise
1 fresh apricot

EVENING
Bean Dip with a selection of crudités
Pasta Crunch

DAY SEVEN
BREAKFAST
As Day One

LUNCH
Eggplant Purée with a selection of
crudités
2 oz. Feta cheese
1 large slice of bread
2 or 3 stalks of celery

EVENING
Mushrooms in Garlic Sauce
6 oz. fish, broiled or baked
Tabbouleh
Tomato Salad

THE VEGETARIAN DIET

THIS PLAN CONTAINS NO MEAT, POULTRY, FISH OR EGGS. THERE ARE SMALL
AMOUNTS OF MILK AND CHEESE IN SOME RECIPES, BUT VEGANS CAN REPLACE
THESE WITH SOY MILK AND TOFU.
ABOUT 1,200 CALORIES PER DAY

Extras per day: 2 glasses (8 oz. each) skim milk or soy milk.

DAY ONE
BREAKFAST
1/2 portion *Mixed Fruit Compote*
1/2 cup skim milk or
soy milk
1/2 grapefruit

LUNCH
Stuffed Bell Peppers
Green Salad

EVENING
3 oz. (dry weight) pasta of choice,
cooked and served with
Walnut Sauce

DAY TWO
BREAKFAST
1/2 grapefruit
1/2 cup *Greek-Style Yogurt*
topped with 1-1/2 oz. dried fruit of
choice and 3 tbsp. muesli

LUNCH
Lentil Soup
1 small slice of bread

EVENING
Mushrooms in Garlic Sauce
Pissaladina
Melon & Strawberry Salad

DAY THREE
BREAKFAST
1 slice of bread with a little low-fat
spread and 2 tsp. honey
1 orange

LUNCH
Tuscan Bean Casserole
Green Salad

EVENING
Tzatziki with a selection of crudités
Vegetable Lasagne
1 banana

DAY FOUR
BREAKFAST
1 oz. (1/3 cup) shelled nuts,
such as almonds
1 peach, nectarine or orange

LUNCH
Tapenade with 1 large piece of toast
Fava Beans & Mushrooms
Lettuce garnish

EVENING
Orange & Fennel Salad
Lentil & Tomato Soup

DAY FIVE
BREAKFAST
As Day One

LUNCH
Red Pepper Soup
1 large slice of bread
Ricotta-Stuffed Tomatoes

EVENING
*Three-Nut Salad with Apricots
& Raisins*
Tabbouleh

DAY SIX
BREAKFAST
As Day Two

LUNCH
Carrot, Apple & Beet Salad
*Fava Bean & Pasta Salad in
Orange Sauce*

EVENING
Tomato & Mushroom Risotto
Peaches in Wine

DAY SEVEN
BREAKFAST
As Day Three

LUNCH
Hummus with 1 pita bread and a
selection of crudités
1 apple

EVENING
3 oz. (dry weight) pasta of
choice, cooked and served with
Tomato Sauce
Baked Pears

THE WEEKEND RELAXER

THIS DIET PLAN CUTS THE CALORIES MOSTLY DURING THE BUSY WORKING WEEK,
BUT ALLOWS YOU TO ENJOY YOURSELF AND EAT A LITTLE MORE ON WEEKENDS.
ABOUT 1,000 CALORIES PER WEEKDAY (DAYS 1 TO 5)
ABOUT 1,700 CALORIES PER DAY ON THE WEEKEND (DAYS 6 & 7)

Extras per day: 2 glasses (8 oz. each) skim milk, 2 glasses (3-1/2 oz. each) medium or dry
wine each day on the weekend.

DAY ONE
BREAKFAST
1 cup *Greek-Style Yogurt*
2 pieces of fresh fruit of choice, such
as apple, pear, peach, nectarine,
orange, grapefruit, or 1 cup soft fruit

LUNCH
2 oz. Feta cheese crumbled on
Tomato Salad
1 pita bread

EVENING
Rice with Bell Peppers & Pork
Lettuce garnish

DAY TWO
BREAKFAST
As Day One

LUNCH
6 oz. fish, broiled
1 large slice of bread
Cucumber slices

EVENING
3 oz. (dry weight) pasta of choice,
cooked and served with
Mushroom Sauce
Lettuce garnish

DAY THREE
BREAKFAST
As Day One

LUNCH
Ricotta-Stuffed Tomatoes
1 large slice of bread

EVENING
Scallops with Mushrooms
1/4 cup rice, cooked
Watercress and lettuce garnish

DAY FOUR
BREAKFAST
As Day One

LUNCH
Melted Mozzarella & Tomato
1 large slice of bread

EVENING
Pasta Crunch
Cucumber slices

DAY FIVE
BREAKFAST
As Day One

LUNCH
Tuna Pita Pockets
1 fresh apricot

EVENING
Mixed Mediterranean Platter
1 banana

DAY SIX
BREAKFAST
As Day One plus
1 slice of bread with a little low-fat
spread and pure fruit spread or honey

LUNCH
Asparagus with Lemon Vinaigrette
Bean Salad
Green Salad

EVENING
Slice of melon
Paella
Peaches in Wine

DAY SEVEN
BREAKFAST
As Day Six

LUNCH
Hummus with a selection of
crudités
Stuffed Bell Peppers

EVENING
Red Pepper Soup
Lamb Pilaf
Citrus & Honey Dessert

THE POST-PREGNANCY DIET

This plan is specifically devised for nursing mothers who would like to lose weight steadily. Those mothers who are not breastfeeding may follow the other low-calorie plans.
ABOUT 1,700 CALORIES PER DAY

Extras per day: 4 or 5 glasses (8 oz. each) skim milk, 1 banana and plenty of low-calorie fluids, especially water.

DAY ONE
BREAKFAST
1 cup fresh fruit juice of choice
1/4 cup muesli with
1/2 cup *Greek-Style Yogurt*

LUNCH
Bean Dip with a selection of crudités
Melted Mozzarella & Tomato
1 slice of bread

EVENING
Lamb Pilaf
Green Salad

DAY TWO
BREAKFAST
Mixed Fruit Compote with
1/4 cup *Greek-Style Yogurt*

LUNCH
Salade Niçoise
1 large slice of bread
1 orange

EVENING
3 oz. (dry weight) pasta of choice, cooked and served with
Lentil Sauce
Green Salad

DAY THREE
BREAKFAST
1 large slice of bread with a little low-fat spread and pure fruit spread or honey
1/2 cup *Greek-Style Yogurt*

LUNCH
Slice of melon
2 oz. Feta cheese
Carrot, Apple & Beet Salad
3 slices of bread

EVENING
Pork Tenderloin Marsala
2 oz. (dry weight) noodles, cooked
1 cup lightly cooked broccoli

DAY FOUR
BREAKFAST
As Day One

LUNCH
Tunisian Eggs
2 slices of bread
1 banana

EVENING
Baked Sea Bass
2 small boiled potatoes
Spinach with Garlic & Oil

DAY FIVE
BREAKFAST
As Day Two

LUNCH
6 oz. fish, pan-fried in a little olive oil
2 slices of bread
Green Salad

EVENING
Vegetable Lasagne
Baked Pears

DAY SIX
BREAKFAST
As Day Three

LUNCH
Tuscan Bean Casserole with 2 tbsp. grated Parmesan cheese

EVENING
Honeyed Chicken
Carrot & Potato Purée
1 cup green beans, lightly cooked

DAY SEVEN
BREAKFAST
As Day One

LUNCH
Lentil Soup
2 slices of bread
1 orange

EVENING
Beef Stiphado
1 (8 oz.) baked potato
2 cups cabbage or other green vegetable, lightly cooked

THE WINTER DIET

THIS PLAN PROVIDES EXTRA CALORIES TO ALLOW YOU TO DIET THROUGH THE
WINTER MONTHS AND ALSO INCLUDES PLENTY OF WARMING DISHES TO KEEP THE
COLD AT BAY.
ABOUT 1,300 CALORIES PER DAY

Extras per day: 2 glasses (8 oz. each) skim milk.

DAY ONE
BREAKFAST
2 slices of toast with a little low-fat
spread and honey
1/2 cup fresh fruit juice of choice

LUNCH
Lentil Soup
1 slice of bread
1 orange

EVENING
Lamb in Yogurt Sauce
1 satsuma

DAY TWO
BREAKFAST
1/2 portion *Mixed Fruit Compote*
1/2 cup hot skim milk
1/2 cup fresh fruit juice of choice

LUNCH
Stuffed Eggplant
5 fresh dates or 1 apple

EVENING
Sardinian Seafood Stew
1 small slice of bread

DAY THREE
BREAKFAST
1/4 cup rolled oats, cooked
with skim milk and mixed with
1 oz. chopped dried fruit of choice
1/2 cup fresh fruit juice of choice

LUNCH
Tuscan Bean Casserole
1 slice of bread
1 orange

EVENING
Rice with Bell Peppers & Pork
Apple & Date Compote

DAY FOUR
BREAKFAST
As Day One

LUNCH
Pissaladina

EVENING
Beef Stiphado
1 (7 oz.) baked potato
1 cup lightly cooked cabbage or
other greens

DAY FIVE
BREAKFAST
As Day Two

LUNCH
Tunisian Eggs
2 slices of bread
1 banana

EVENING
3 oz. (dry weight) spaghetti, cooked
and served with
Lentil Sauce

DAY SIX
BREAKFAST
As Day Three

LUNCH
Minestrone Soup
2 slices of bread
1 orange

EVENING
Lamb & Apricot Casserole
3 tbsp. rice, cooked

DAY SEVEN
BREAKFAST
As Day One

LUNCH
1/2 portion *Hummus* with a selection
of crudités
6 oz. fish, broiled
1 large slice of bread

EVENING
Chicken with 30 Cloves of Garlic
Carrot & Potato Purée
1 cup lightly cooked cabbage or
other greens

THE SUMMER SIZZLER

WITH LITTLE COOKING AND PLENTY OF APPEALING SALADS, THIS DIET IS IDEAL
FOR THOSE SUMMER MONTHS WHEN THE HEAT IS ON.
ABOUT 1,200 CALORIES PER DAY

Extras per day: 2 glasses (8 oz. each) skim milk, 1 glass (3-1/2 oz.) chilled white wine or
champagne.

DAY THREE
BREAKFAST
As Day One

LUNCH
Melted Mozzarella & Tomato
1 large slice of bread
1 apple

EVENING
Mushrooms in Garlic Sauce
Bean Salad
Green Salad
1 cup strawberries with 2 tbsp.
Greek-Style Yogurt and 1 tsp. sugar

DAY FOUR
BREAKFAST
As Day One

LUNCH
*Fava Bean & Pasta Salad in Orange
Sauce*
1 nectarine

EVENING
*Three-Nut Salad with Apricots &
Raisins*
Banana & Strawberry Sorbets

DAY FIVE
BREAKFAST
As Day One

LUNCH
Tuna Pita Pockets
1 cup grapes or strawberries

EVENING
Mixed Mediterranean Platter
Peaches in Wine

DAY SIX
BREAKFAST
As Day One

LUNCH
Seafood Salad with Citrus Dressing
1 peach

EVENING
2-1/2 oz. (dry weight) pasta of
choice, cooked and served with
Pesto
Lettuce dinner salad

DAY SEVEN
BREAKFAST
As Day One

LUNCH
Tabbouleh
2 oz. cooked chicken
1 banana

EVENING
Shrimp Salad

DAY ONE
BREAKFAST
1 cup *Greek-Style Yogurt*
2 portions of fresh fruit from the
following: 1 nectarine, 1 peach,
2 plums, 1 mango, 1 orange,
1 grapefruit, 1 large slice of melon,
1 cup cherries, strawberries or
raspberries

LUNCH
Feta Pita Pockets

EVENING
Salade Niçoise
1 large slice of bread
Melon & Strawberry Salad

DAY TWO
BREAKFAST
As Day One

LUNCH
Tapenade with a selection of crudités
Crab & Melon Salad

EVENING
Avocado with Mâche
1 large slice of bread
Citrus & Honey Dessert

THE MEDITERRANEAN KITCHEN

Changing from the Western to the Mediterranean style of eating will involve some quite different patterns of shopping and stocking the cupboard. This chapter takes a good look at some of the most important Mediterranean ingredients and advises on buying and storage.

If you are changing to a Mediterranean diet, you will need to do a certain amount of rethinking and restocking in the kitchen. Foods that have formed a small part of your meals will now form a large part; and foods previously much used will now be relegated to an occasional role.

In this chapter I will take you through the contents of your new pantry and refrigerator and give a guide to what ingredients you will need as permanent stock, where to buy them, and which varieties to buy, where appropriate. Despite its great reliance on fresh produce, having a good, varied store is one of the most important parts of the Mediterranean kitchen. Dried foods, preserved foods, and even cans are traditionally a big part of the Mediterranean cook's kitchen, and staples are always readily available to make up a quick meal, not just at the times when fresh produce is in short supply but all year round as well.

A few years ago it was hard to find all the necessary ingredients for Mediterranean cooking in North America, unless you lived, for example, within shopping distance of a major downtown area with a myriad of ethnic grocers tucked away down its side streets. Now it becomes easier every year to find what you want; if the supermarket doesn't have it, the local gourmet food store certainly will. Perhaps the hardest thing to find is a good choice of Mediterranean fish and shellfish. However, acceptable alternatives can usually be found.

Necessary kitchen utensils will probably not vary much from those you already have in your home. However, you can invest in authentic pasta pans and couscousières, etc. if you wish to.

THE PANTRY
OLIVE OIL is the perfect oil for all cooking and salad dressing needs as there are so many different varieties, each with their own particular character.

It may be heated safely to very high temperatures

OPPOSITE: Raspberries in wine vinegar and extra virgin olive oil

and, in tests, food fried in olive oil absorbs at least 12% less oil than food fried in other oils or fats. You therefore get a lighter finished dish, and of course fewer calories.

Olive oils from Spain, Italy and Greece are widely available here. Italian olive oil is considered the best by many. Of course, the Greeks, Spanish, and other olive oil producers would *not* agree! Within each country there are also various distinctive regional varieties of oils. For instance, within Italy, some connoisseurs prefer the oil of Tuscany, while others say that Liguria oil is superior. However, like a wine buff, the olive oil connoisseur will take years to learn his or her preferences and know the oils well. If you are a beginner, it is important to know the different qualities of oil.

Virgin olive oil comes from the first pressing of the olives. You may also see the words "first pressing" or "cold pressed" on the label. Some labels will state that the oil is *extra virgin*–this means that it has no more than 1% acidity, whereas "virgin" oil may have up to 3.3% acidity. If any olive oil isn't virgin, it will simply be labeled *pure olive oil* and will come from a later pressing of the olives. There may be several pressings and usually the least expensive olive oils will be from the last pressings.

Although the color and flavor of olive oils varies very much from country to country , olive to olive, and year to year, broadly the virgin oils are usually a more distinctive greener, and/or richer golden color, with a stronger distinctive, richer and more fruity taste. They are ideal for salad dressings, and for using neat on pasta, bread, etc.

The oil of the later pressings will usually be a lighter color: pale yellow or gold, with a lighter taste. These oils are good for frying and sautéing and for casseroles, etc. If you find the taste of virgin oil *too* strong–which some people do–you may actually prefer to use a "pure olive oil" for all purposes.

I suggest that, to begin with, you buy one virgin or extra-virgin oil and one later pressing oil–as you use up each bottle you can try a different brand next time, until you discover the ones you prefer. For this reason it is best at first to buy olive oil in smaller bottles rather, say, than the huge cans you can find in some grocers!

Most supermarkets now stock at least a few vari-eties of olive oil. You may find more choice in any gourmet store, or perhaps a natural-food store. Alternatively, if you live in a city, a department store's kitchenware section may stock good oils.

· Keep your olive oil in a cool, dark place and it will last for a long time–not that it needs to!

WINE VINEGAR is used by Mediterranean cooks much as we use distilled vinegar. So abandon your white vinegar and stock up with red and white wine vinegar, either plain or flavored with herbs for variety. I prefer red wine vinegar for its richer color and flavor, but white wine vinegar is perfectly suitable both for cooking and for dressings, especially with fish and poultry dishes. An easy way to impart garlic flavor to salad is to steep crushed cloves in the vinegar before making your dressing.

PASTA may be made at home if you have a lot of spare time and, preferably, a pasta machine. Alternatively, you can do what most people do and buy dried pasta, which I find perfectly acceptable and many people actually prefer. Buy only 100% durum wheat pasta. Don't buy any other kind as it won't give you that nice firm, unsticky, *al dente* texture, and will all too often cook to a mush. If you can't find the words "100% durum wheat" on the label of pasta, just don't buy it. I think pasta made in Italy is the best.

Whole-wheat pasta contains a little more fiber than durum wheat pasta, but I find the texture and taste poor in comparison. Ordinary durum wheat pasta contains wheat germ, which is a plus. If you prefer whole-wheat, it can be used in any of the recipes in this book, but it will need longer cooking.

Ready-made fresh pasta is available in the cold food section at many supermarkets. The quality of such pasta varies tremendously. If you find a good source, don't forget that it only needs a few minutes of cooking.

There are many different shapes of pasta. In Italy you will find at least 100 and probably more. In the US, there is a reasonable choice at supermarkets and if you have an Italian grocer near you, the choice will be even greater.

The Italians select their pasta shapes according to what will go best with the sauce. For instance, long spaghetti is best served with a sauce which contains no large pieces and is fairly liquid so that it will cling to the pasta–tomato sauce or plain olive oil and Parmesan are ideal. Shells and short shapes suit heavier sauces with larger chunks of food in it, and hollow pasta likes a creamy sauce that will run inside it as well as cling to it.

Apart from plain pasta you can also buy green pasta, which is colored with spinach, and red pasta made with tomato. These add a little extra flavor, but the addition of color to the plate is perhaps the main reason that these pastas are used. They are also pretty in salads, and if your sauce is a neutral color, like walnut or mushroom, a green or red pasta will look more appetizing.

Experiment with your own pasta shapes, colors and combinations. Whatever you do, learn to cook pasta well. It hates to be overcooked and/or kept waiting around as it loses heat very quickly.

Boil plenty of lightly salted water in a large pan, then add a dash of olive oil to prevent the pasta sticking together. Test a small piece of pasta a minute before the end of cooking time stated on the package. When *al dente*–tender but still firm to the bite–remove the pasta from the heat immediately, drain and serve promptly.

RICE & GRAINS are staples of the region. Rice is the principal grain used throughout the Mediterranean, apart from North Africa where couscous is favored. The Mediterraneans frequently use *short-grain rice* for savory dishes in addition to the special short-grain *Arborio* or *risotto rice*. You can use short-grain or risotto rice for paella, but I prefer *long-grain rice* and even sometimes use the Indian *basmati rice* for its fuller flavor.

The Mediterraneans don't make much use of *brown rice*, but you can use it in salad recipes and side dishes if you prefer. It does not work well in risottos, pilafs or paellas, as it tends to remain firm to the bite and doesn't absorb the liquids of the dish as it should.

Couscous is the grain of Morocco and Tunisia. It is made from hard wheat, and you can generally buy it in natural-food stores and supermarkets. It is simply soaked to swell it up and then steamed over the stew with which it is to be served. A little goes a long way, as it swells greatly during cooking.

Bulgur is an Eastern Mediterranean pre-cooked coarsely ground wheat. It is first soaked for a few minutes and then used in salads such as *Tabbouleh*. It, too, is available from natural-food stores and most supermarkets.

LEGUMES, such as dried beans, peas and lentils, are widely used throughout the Mediterranean. They can be put into salads and are frequently used as the bases for soups and stews. They may also be used to make sauces and dips, or they can be served on their own as a hot side dish, perhaps flavored with herbs or tomatoes.

Although you can buy dried legumes in packages from the supermarket, which will probably have a small selection of the most popular types, I prefer to go to a natural-food store for mine. This is not only because the selection will be larger, but because you can buy in bulk. As legumes keep for a long time stored in dry conditions, this makes a great deal of financial sense.

It is also worth buying some canned beans. As they are pre-cooked, if you forget to soak your dried beans you have a quick standby. Also, I find canned chickpeas, for instance, much nicer than dried ones when making *Hummus*, and canned red kidney beans are certainly as nice as the dried ones.

Dried beans, especially chickpeas and kidney beans, need to be soaked for several hours or overnight. The soaking water is then discarded and the beans boiled rapidly in fresh water for 10 minutes to remove toxins. The beans are then simmered for an hour or two until tender. It is important not to add salt to legumes until they are cooked as it makes them tough.

The best lentils to buy are the small brown ones (my favorites) or the green ones, in preference to the orange ones which have less flavor. Lentils do not need pre-soaking.

Not all beans taste the same. The following are some the Mediterraneans enjoy regularly:

Borlotti bean: a pale, pinkish-brown Italian bean used in salads and casseroles.

Broad or fava bean: these are brown if they still have their skins and white if the skin has been removed; they make good salads and soups.

Cannellini bean: creamy white bean used in classic Italian dishes.

OVERLEAF: The Mediterranean pantry

Chickpea or garbanzo bean: these hard round "peas" are popular in North Africa and the Eastern Mediterranean.

Flageolet: pretty pale-green bean, similar to a small lima bean.

Haricot or navy bean: the most common Mediterranean bean, small and white, used in casseroles and very good with lamb and pork dishes.

Kidney bean: these go into Italian soups and salads, and are included in casseroles throughout the Mediterranean.

DRIED FRUITS, such as apricots, peaches, figs, prunes, dates and raisins, may all be found in the Mediterranean region and they are used in cooking all the time– in hot fruit dishes, in savory dishes and salads, with yogurt, or just as a snack on their own. Here you can buy small boxes or packages of dried fruit at the supermarket, but you may cut costs and also find more variety at the natural-food store. Remember that dried fruit should always be stored in airtight containers.

NUTS & SEEDS are much favored in Mediterranean cooking. For value, these are best bought loose from the natural-food store rather than in the small packages you normally get in the supermarkets. However, don't buy too many nuts at once as they do lose flavor and become dry if kept more than a few weeks, shelled or unshelled.

Almonds: a particular favorite in Spain where they are used in a variety of dishes, whole, toasted or ground.

Pine nuts: are a classic ingredient of Mediterranean cooking. They have a distinctive taste which no other nut can match, and a soft, melting texture. They are available here, but are not easy to obtain everywhere as some grocers consider them too expensive to stock. However, a few of these nuts go a long way, and I have managed to persuade my local grocer to order some especially for me. If a minimum order is too much for you, arrange to split it among some of your friends.

Walnuts: make fabulous sauces and are one of my favorite salad additions. For sauces you can buy the less costly walnut pieces rather than halves.

Sesame seeds: are widely used sprinkled on vegetables or sweet dishes, or ground into the famous tahini paste of Greece and the Lebanon.

Sunflower seeds: make a nutritious snack or addition to a breakfast muesli.

CANS & JARS are very useful, even if fresh or dried natural ingredients are so important in Mediterranean cooking. There are a few cans, jars or tubes that I advise you to stock your pantry with, without any need to feel that you are not staying true to the spirit of this cuisine.

Fish: you will be hard-pressed to find fresh or frozen anchovies in this country and it is also not always easy to find fresh or frozen tuna, so I suggest you stock up with some cans of both. Buy tuna in oil rather than tuna in brine or water which, although it contains fewer calories, has probably lost most of its Omega-3 oils. If you drain the fish well, the calorie count won't actually be much higher.

Tomatoes: you will find canned tomatoes mentioned in many of the recipes in this book. This is because Italian plum tomatoes are full of flavor and very versatile and, unless you can get such very ripe, very tasty, true Mediterranean tomatoes, I think canned tomatoes work better. Under-ripe, pale tomatoes are no substitute. Also buy tomato paste, preferably the kind with no added salt.

Tahini: buy a jar of tahini, preferably the light tahini. You could possibly make your own, but I am sure you could make it no better.

Honey: a jar of Greek honey on your shelf is an absolute must!

Olives: you can buy olives either ripe or green, with or without pits, stuffed or plain, packed in jars, cans or vacuum-sealed. My own preference is for pitted ripe olives, either in jars or vacuum packs. Go for the largest, plumpest olives you can find, and rinse them before you use them to take away some of the saltiness. Serve olives with aperitifs, as part of a selection of *mezes* or *tapas* or on their own. You can also use them as a garnish on salads.

HERBS are the heart of Mediterranean cooking. It is a pity for most of us that we can't walk to a nearby hillside and pick wild thyme, rosemary, parsley, basil or cilantro as many Mediterraneans still can. Although dried herbs bought from the supermarket can be a reasonable substitute, fresh is almost always best. If you have a garden or patio, consider starting a herb plot as most herbs are quite easy to grow and thrive throughout the summer in a sunny spot. Otherwise, look for fresh herbs at supermarkets and specialty food stores.

I know dried herbs in glass jars look pretty in the kitchen, but if you do have to buy dried this is absolutely the worst way to store them if you still want them to taste or smell of anything in a week or two. The rule with dried herbs is to buy in small quantities and store them away from heat and light to retain their flavor and aroma.

The following are the most widely used Mediterranean herbs:

Basil: one of Italy's favorites and particularly good with tomatoes. Easy to grow. The dried herb is strong, so use sparingly.

Bay leaf: sweet herb which does dry and keep well. Ideal with lamb and fish and in stews.

Chives: these do not dry well but can easily be grown on a windowsill. Fresh chopped chives are a wonderful garnish for salads and soups.

Cilantro leaves (also called Coriander and Chinese parsley): chop for salads and use whole leaves for garnishes.

Garlic: hardly a herb, in Mediterranean terms, as so much is used. Buy the biggest, firmest bulbs you can find. It is worth buying a whole rope of good garlic. Hang it in a cool, dry place and it will keep for months.

Marjoram: good in tomato dishes. Dries well.

Mint: fresh mint is used in *Tabbouleh* and *Tzatziki*, and as a garnish. Does not dry well.

Oregano: one of my favorite herbs. Fresh or dried, it is quite delicious in tomato dishes and sauces, and in stews.

Parsley: our parsley is usually curly-leaved, but the Mediterranean version is flat-leaved and has a distinctively different flavor. If you can't find it, the curly kind will do.

Rosemary: this is a classic Italian herb for all lamb and pork dishes; use sparingly. Dries quite well.

Thyme: use on chicken and lamb before roasting or grilling, or sprinkle some of the tiny leaves into lamb casseroles. Dries well.

SPICES, with few exceptions, are best bought whole and ground as you need them. Bought ready-ground, spices quickly lose their flavor and aroma. With a pestle and mortar or spice mill, you can grind the exact amount you need as and when you need it.

Allspice: adds a warm flavor to casseroles.

Capers: pickled buds which may need rinsing before use to remove excess saltiness.

Chiles: buy fresh or dried. Remove seeds before mincing or chopping. Dried chiles are often hotter than fresh ones–and the very small chiles are often the hottest of all!

Cinnamon: used either ground or in stick form in pilafs and Moroccan dishes.

Paprika: sweet and red, it adds depth, color and warmth to many casseroles and stews.

Pepper: black peppercorns are best.

Saffron: expensive, so save for paellas and other authentic Spanish dishes. Buy the strands if possible, rather than the powder, and soak them in a very little water before using. Add both strands and water to the dish.

Turmeric: can give a saffron color to a dish but the flavor is totally different and much harsher.

BREAD

The one thing I crave and can't get anywhere near where I live is bread that reminds me of the wonderful breads of Spain, Italy and Greece. I suppose the nearest you can get is a stone-ground whole-wheat or rye bread, or a homemade loaf. Never, never use ordinary sliced white bread–it just won't do!

CHEESE

You can buy many Mediterranean cheeses now at larger supermarkets. For the recipes in this book, you will need Feta from Greece, Ricotta and Mozzarella from Italy – and of course, Parmesan. Parmesan is a high-fat cheese, but a little goes a long way when it is grated. Always buy Parmesan in a piece and grate it yourself; the flavor is infinitely superior to ready-grated cheese. Wrap the piece in foil and it will keep a long time in the refrigerator.

If you want a cheese for eating with bread and salad, buy a medium-fat cheese.

FISH

Many of the most well-known Mediterranean fishes are available in some parts of the US, but if your local fish merchant doesn't appear to stock anything other than cod and flounder, ask him if he can order other fish for you. Shop around and buy when

prices are low; you can always freeze any surplus. Among my favorite white fish, though on the expensive side, are swordfish and monkfish, and my favorites for baking and grilling are mackerel, sardines and red mullet.

You can't buy a decent fish stock in a cube and it is so easy to make your own as the base of Mediterranean fish stews and soups. Just ask the fish merchant for the heads, tails and bones of fish and simmer them in water with chopped celery, carrot, leek, onion and some seasoning for 30 minutes–no more! Strain, reduce the liquid if necessary, then refrigerate or freeze. You can freeze very concentrated stock directly into an ice cube tray for dishes where you need only a small amount of flavoring.

FRUITS & VEGETABLES

In recent years our supermarkets and local grocers have recognized our craving for new varieties of fruit and vegetables, and so now virtually everything that the Mediterraneans enjoy, you can also find here.

When buying, always choose the freshest produce you can. Buy from a market that keeps its fruit and vegetables away from heat and sunlight. Refuse anything that is bruised, blackened, damaged, or wrinkled. Fruits and vegetables quickly lose their vitamin C when badly stored or handled, or if kept too long. Once home, store them in cool, dark conditions and use them as quickly as possible–buy little and often.

UTENSILS

Although you can easily cook almost all of the recipes in this book using equipment you undoubtedly already have at home, once you get the Mediterranean "bug" you may like to buy a few pieces to make your life easier.

If you enjoy paella and intend to make it regularly, the first thing I suggest you buy is a large two-handled paella pan. Even the largest skillet is not really adequate for a full paella serving four or more people, so you may have the bother of cooking in two separate pans.

OPPOSITE: Mediterranean herbs, spices and aromatic flavorings

A pestle and mortar is useful for grinding small amounts of spices. Electric spice mills often don't work well with small quantities and it is so much better to grind your spices as you need them.

You may like a garlic press, though the job is done almost as well between the flat side of a metal spatula or knife on a chopping board.

Long, slow cooking is the secret of success for many Mediterranean stews and casseroles, and for this you ideally need a cast-iron Dutch oven with a really tight-fitting lid.

As so much Mediterranean cooking involves much chopping and preparation, a set of good kitchen knives is a must and they should be kept well sharpened. I always prefer to use a good sharp knife for chopping fresh herbs rather than a mill or food processor.

THE RECIPES

The recipes which follow are a selection of my favorites. All recipes serve four, but quantities for most can easily be cut or expanded to suit your numbers.

Apart from the fact that the recipes should form part of a healthy diet as described in earlier chapters my criterion when selecting them was that they should either be very easy, or at least fairly easy, to prepare and cook. After all, most of us are busy people and are not professional cooks, and that includes me! We like to provide good food and we like to entertain, but we don't have too many hours to spend doing so.

The recipes had to offer variety and they had to look nice. Most importantly, they had to taste wonderful and be satisfying.

However, don't be afraid to rely on very simple meals, such as basic pastas with plain sauces or grilled or baked fish with a few herbs and a side salad. Mediterranean food can be suitably grand when you want it to be for special occasions–or as simple as you like.

My main hope is that eating a Mediterranean-style meal–whether you have eaten it alone or, as the Mediterranean people themselves prefer to do, in the company of good friends or family on a shady terrace–will leave you smiling and feeling completely content.

TAPENADE
France

Tapenade keeps well in the refrigerator and is traditionally served with toast.

Calories per serving: 152
Saturated fat: Low
Protein: Low
Carbohydrate: Low
Fiber: 3 g
Cholesterol: Negligible
Vitamins: C
Minerals: Iron, Calcium

1-1/3 cups pitted ripe olives (8 oz.)
1-1/2 tbsp. capers
1 anchovy fillet
1/4 cup olive oil
1 tsp. lemon juice
1/2 tsp. Dijon-style mustard
1 small garlic clove, crushed
1/2 tsp. chopped bay leaf

If the olives were packed in brine, rinse them well. Soak the capers in water 20 minutes to reduce their saltiness.

Blend all ingredients to a paste in a blender or food processor.

TZATZIKI
Greece

Perfect as a light appetizer with crudités, tzatziki is also often served as a side dish, especially with spicy lamb dishes.

Calories per serving: 68
Saturated fat: Low
Protein: High
Carbohydrate: Low
Fiber: Trace
Cholesterol: 3.5 mg
Vitamins: Niacin
Minerals: Calcium

1 garlic clove, minced
4-inch piece of cucumber, finely
  chopped
2-1/4 cups *Greek-Style Yogurt* (see
  page 124)
Salt and black pepper
Handful of fresh mint leaves,
  chopped

Mix the garlic and cucumber into the yogurt, season lightly and chill.

Serve sprinkled with the mint.

EGGPLANT PURÉE
Greece

Yogurt is sometimes added to this dish, but I prefer the richer taste of my version.

Calories per serving: 85
Saturated fat: Low
Protein: Low
Carbohydrate: Low
Fiber: 5 g
Cholesterol: Nil
Vitamins: C, Folic acid
Minerals: Iron

2 large eggplants
3 tbsp. olive oil
2 large garlic cloves, crushed
3–4 tbsp. lemon juice
Salt and black pepper
Pinch of paprika (optional), for
  garnish

Bake the eggplants in the oven preheated to 375F (190C) until their skins are charred and the insides are soft, about 45 minutes

Discard the skins and place the flesh in a blender or food processor with the oil, garlic, 2 tablespoons of the lemon juice, and a little salt and pepper. Purée to a smooth paste, then taste and add more lemon juice and salt if necessary. Garnish with a little paprika, if using.

CARROT & POTATO PURÉE
—— *Italy* ——

Delicious with crusty bread, this purée may also be served as a side dish to accompany a main course. It is important to use waxy, not mealy, potatoes.

Calories per serving: 140
Saturated fat: Low
Protein: Low
Carbohydrate: High
Fiber: 3.5 g
Cholesterol: Nil
Vitamins: Beta-carotene, C
Minerals: Potassium, Iron

3/4 lb. potatoes (see left), peeled and sliced
3/4 lb. carrots, peeled and sliced
2 garlic cloves, peeled
3 tbsp. olive oil
1-1/2 tbsp. lemon juice
4 tsp. ground cumin
Pinch of cayenne pepper
Salt and black pepper

Cook the potatoes and carrots with the garlic cloves in lightly salted boiling water until they are tender.

Drain and mash with the oil. Stir in the lemon juice, cumin, and cayenne and season to taste. Serve warm or cold.

HUMMUS
—— *Greece* ——

Canned chickpeas give a lighter hummus, which I prefer, but you can use the dried variety.

Calories per serving: 164
Saturated fat: Low
Protein: Medium
Carbohydrate: Low
Fiber: 2 g
Cholesterol: Nil
Vitamins: A, C, E, Niacin
Minerals. Iron, Potassium, Calcium

2/3 cup canned chickpeas (garbanzo beans) *or*
  1/4 cup dried chickpeas
1/4 cup light tahini
2 garlic cloves, crushed
Juice of 2 lemons
Salt
Paprika, for garnish

If using canned chickpeas, rinse and drain them. If using dried chickpeas, soak them overnight. Drain and boil in fresh water 10 minutes, then simmer 1 or 2 hours until tender. Drain.

Purée all the ingredients in a blender or food processor. Serve at room temperature with paprika sprinkled over the top.

BEAN DIP
—— *Italy* ——

Fresh tender, young beans are needed for this dish.

Calories per serving: 130
Saturated fat: Low
Protein: Low
Carbohydrate: Low
Fiber: 2.5 g
Cholesterol: 2 mg
Vitamins: Beta-carotene, C
Minerals: Iron, Calcium

1/2 lb. shelled fresh fava or lima beans (1-1/2 cups)
2 garlic cloves, crushed
3 tbsp. grated Parmesan cheese
1/4 cup olive oil

Cook the beans in lightly salted boiling water until tender. Drain well.

Blend all ingredients to a purée in a blender or food processor, reserving a few beans.

Garnish with the reserved beans and drizzle over a little more oil.

ROASTED YELLOW PEPPER DIP
—————— Spain ——————

This unusual dip can be spread on toast and warmed under the broiler to make a quick snack.

Calories per serving: 198
Saturated fat: Medium
Protein: High
Carbohydrate: Low
Fiber: 0.5 g
Cholesterol: 24 mg
Vitamins: Beta-carotene, C
Minerals: Calcium

2 yellow bell peppers
4 oz. Feta or goat cheese
5 oz. low-fat cream cheese
3 tbsp. olive oil
Salt and black pepper

Cook the peppers under the broiler until they are blackened all over. Remove the skins under running water, then pat the peppers dry.

Remove core and seeds and chop the peppers coarsely. Purée them with the cheeses in a blender or food processor, then add the oil little by little with the machine still running. Season to taste.

The dip will keep several days in the refrigerator.

LENTIL SOUP
—————— France ——————

There are a thousand ways to make lentil soup, but this is my particular favorite.

Calories per serving: 310
Saturated fat: Low
Protein: High
Carbohydrate: High
Fiber: 11.5 g
Cholesterol: Nil
Vitamins: C, Beta-carotene
Minerals: Iron

2 tbsp. olive oil
1 onion, chopped
1 leek, trimmed and chopped
1-3/4 cups green lentils
1 quart vegetable stock
1 celery stalk, chopped
1 carrot, chopped
2 garlic cloves, crushed
1 bay leaf
1-1/2 tbsp. chopped parsley
Salt and black pepper

Heat the oil in a heavy-based saucepan over medium heat and sauté the onion and leek until soft.

Add the lentils and stir. Pour in the stock and bring to a boil. Reduce the heat and add the remaining ingredients. Simmer about 1 hour, until the lentils are soft. Adjust the seasoning.

The texture of this soup may be varied by puréeing some of it in a blender or food processor and then returning this purée to the pan. The result is a thick soup which still has some texture.

PREVIOUS PAGES: Bean Dip (page 59); Roasted Yellow Pepper Dip (page 62); Hummus (page 59); Tapenade (page 58); RIGHT: Lentil Soup

MINESTRONE SOUP
—— *Italy* ——

Homemade minestrone is a healthy feast which is not to be missed. Well-flavored stock is essential.

Calories per serving: 190
Saturated fat: Low
Protein: High
Carbohydrate: Low
Fiber: 6 g
Cholesterol: 9 mg
Vitamins: C, Beta-carotene, Niacin
Minerals: Calcium, Potassium, Iron

1 large onion
2 leeks
3 celery stalks
2 carrots
6 oz. white cabbage
1-1/2 tbsp. olive oil
2 oz. lean bacon or pancetta, finely chopped
1 cup canned tomatoes
2 garlic cloves, crushed
Salt and black pepper
1 quart chicken or ham stock
1 tbsp. chopped fresh basil
2 oz. pasta shapes
1-1/2 tsp. tomato paste
3 tbsp. chopped parsley
1/3 cup grated Parmesan cheese, for garnish

Finely chop all the vegetables.

Heat the oil in a large saucepan over medium heat and sauté the bacon 2 minutes. Add the onion and sauté until soft. Add the celery, carrots, tomatoes, garlic and seasoning, cover and simmer gently 20 minutes, stirring occasionally.

Pour in the stock and basil and simmer 1 hour. Add the leeks, pasta and cabbage and simmer 30 minutes. Stir in the tomato paste and simmer 10 minutes longer. Stir in the parsley and garnish with the Parmesan cheese.

Variations: Zucchini can be used instead of the cabbage. Cooked navy beans can be used instead of the pasta, in which case the fiber content will go up to 9 g per serving.

RED PEPPER SOUP
—— *Spain* ——

Served well chilled, this dish makes a change from gazpacho.

Calories per serving: 38
Saturated fat: Low
Protein: Medium
Carbohydrate: High
Fiber: 2 g
Cholesterol: Nil
Vitamins: Beta-carotene, C
Minerals: Potassium, Iron

2 very large or 4 small red bell peppers
1 (15-oz.) can tomatoes
1 small garlic clove, crushed
Salt and black pepper
A little tomato juice
1-1/2 tbsp. chopped parsley, for garnish

Cook the peppers under the broiler until they are blackened all over. Remove the skins under running water and pat dry.

Remove core and seeds and chop the flesh, then purée it in a blender or food processor along with the tomatoes, garlic, and seasoning to taste. If the soup is a little thick, dilute it with tomato juice.

Serve chilled, garnished with the parsley. Alternatively, use chopped raw red or green bell peppers.

CRAB & MELON SALAD
—— *Italy* ——

Calories per serving: 96
Saturated fat: Low
Protein: High
Carbohydrate: Low
Fiber: 1.25 g
Cholesterol: 50 mg
Vitamins: Beta-carotene, C
Minerals: Potassium, Calcium, Iron

4 chicory leaves
1 cantaloupe melon
Meat from 1 large freshly cooked crab
1-1/2 tbsp. olive oil
1-1/2 tbsp. lemon juice
Black pepper

Arrange the chicory leaves on four serving plates. Peel and seed the melon. Slice it into half moon shapes and divide these among the plates.

Divide the crab meat among the plates, then drizzle on the oil and lemon juice and sprinkle with plenty of black pepper.

MUSHROOMS IN GARLIC SAUCE
———— *France* ————

Calories per serving: 67
Saturated fat: Low
Protein: Low
Carbohydrate: Trace
Fiber: 1.5 g
Cholesterol: Nil
Vitamins: Niacin
Minerals: Potassium

1/2 lb. mushrooms
3 tbsp. olive oil
3 garlic cloves, minced
Juice of 1/2 lemon
Salt and black pepper
3 tbsp. chopped parsley, for garnish

Wipe the mushrooms clean, but don't get them too wet. Leave the caps whole and chop the stems finely.

Heat the oil in a pan over high heat and add the mushroom caps along with the stems and the garlic. Sauté 2 or 3 minutes.

Add the lemon juice and season to taste. Serve hot or cold sprinkled with the parsley.

RICOTTA-STUFFED TOMATOES
———— *Italy* ————

Cottage or low-fat cream cheese works equally well in this recipe.

Calories per serving: 187
Saturated fat: Medium
Protein: High
Carbohydrate: Low
Fiber: 4 g
Cholesterol: 19 mg
Vitamins: Beta-carotene, C
Minerals: Calcium, Potassium

4 large tomatoes
1 cup Ricotta cheese
1/2 cup chopped walnuts
3 tbsp. chopped parsley
2 mushrooms, finely chopped
3 tbsp. whole-wheat bread crumbs
Black pepper
4 ripe olives, for garnish

Preheat the oven to 350F (175C).

Cut the top quarter off each tomato. Scoop out the flesh and chop this and the tops; place in a bowl. Add the cheese, nuts, parsley, mushrooms, bread crumbs and pepper. Beat together well.

Pile the mixture into the tomato shells. Place in a shallow ovenproof dish and bake 30 minutes. Garnish with the olives and serve.

TUSCAN BEAN CASSEROLE
———— *Italy* ————

You can use canned beans as a shortcut in this recipe, or use all navy beans if you prefer.

Calories per serving: 280
Saturated fat: Low
Protein: High
Carbohydrate: High
Fiber: 21 g
Cholesterol: Nil
Vitamins: Thiamin, E
Minerals: Potassium, Iron

1 cup dried navy beans
1 cup dried red kidney beans
2 tbsp. olive oil
1 large garlic clove, chopped
1 cup chopped canned tomatoes
2 tsp. chopped fresh sage
Salt and black pepper
1-1/2 tbsp. chopped parsley, for garnish

Soak the beans overnight. Drain them, put them in a pan and cover them with water. Bring to a boil and boil 10 minutes, then lower the heat and simmer 1 hour or more until tender. Drain.

Heat the oil in a skillet over high heat and sauté the garlic a few seconds. Add the cooked beans, tomatoes and sage with salt and pepper to taste. Cover and simmer a few minutes, adding water or tomato juice if the mixture looks too dry.

Serve hot or cold, sprinkled with the chopped parsley.

FAVA BEANS & MUSHROOMS
—— *Italy* ——

Cèpes are good in this dish, but use whatever mushrooms you can find.

Calories per serving: 92
Saturated fat: Low
Protein: Medium
Carbohydrate: Low
Fiber: 4.5 g
Cholesterol: Negligible
Vitamins: C, Beta-carotene, Niacin
Minerals: Potassium, Iron

10 oz. shelled fresh fava or lima beans (2 cups)
2 tbsp. olive oil
10 oz. fresh cèpes or other mushrooms, sliced if large
1 garlic clove
1 tsp. dried oregano
Little lemon juice
Salt and black pepper
3 tbsp. *Greek-Style Yogurt* (see page 124)

Cook the beans in lightly salted boiling water until just tender.

Heat the oil in a skillet over medium heat and stir-fry the mushrooms and garlic 2 minutes. Add the well-drained beans along with the oregano and lemon juice. Season to taste and fry 2 more minutes, stirring all the time.

Pile the mixture into a serving dish and spoon over the yogurt.

ASPARAGUS WITH LEMON VINAIGRETTE
—— *Italy* ——

Asparagus is rich in many vitamins and minerals. Choose plump spears rather than long thin ones.

Calories per serving: 150
Saturated fat: Medium
Protein: High
Carbohydrate: Low
Fiber: 2.5 g
Cholesterol: 4.5 mg
Vitamins: Beta-carotene, C, E, Folic acid
Minerals: Potassium, Iron, Calcium

24 asparagus spears (see left)
1/4 cup olive oil
Juice of 1 lemon
Pinch of grated nutmeg
Salt and black pepper
1/3 cup grated Parmesan cheese

Tie the asparagus into four bundles with string. Place them, tips uppermost, in a tall pan containing 2 inches of water. Steam the asparagus 10 minutes or until the spears are tender.

Meanwhile, blend the oil, lemon juice and nutmeg together well with salt and pepper to taste.

Arrange the asparagus spears on warmed plates. Pour the vinaigrette over the asparagus and sprinkle with the cheese.

OPPOSITE: Asparagus with Lemon Vinaigrette; Fava Beans & Mushrooms

LUNCHES & SUPPERS

Mediterranean eating is, above all, a relaxed way of eating. So if you are searching for an informal supper just for one,

a quick meal for the family or an easy-to-prepare lunch for friends, you'll find plenty of good suggestions for all these in this chapter.

The essence of a supper or a lunch is informality. Whatever you choose to cook, the result should be something that can be eaten from one plate, perhaps on your knee using just a fork, and with no need for any accompaniment—apart from a glass of wine or a salad garnish.

Supper dishes should also be either quick or easy to prepare. Hence most of the recipes in this chapter will appeal to the cook in a hurry as well as to the inexperienced chef. Many of the dishes are also inexpensive, and most are suitable for vegetarians.

If you are eating alone, several recipes can be scaled down to serve one—particularly the *Pita Pockets*, the *Melted Mozzarella & Tomato*, the *Tunisian Eggs* and the *Lamb in Yogurt Sauce*.

The easiest of all Mediterranean suppers is a plate of fresh sardines, either pan-fried in a little olive oil, or brushed with oil and broiled or barbecued, and served sprinkled with lemon juice and black pepper. Another very simple and quick dish is some Feta cheese crumbled over a sliced ripe tomato, topped with chopped parsley and eaten with warmed pita bread.

I have included some dishes that take slightly longer to prepare, simply because of their "deliciousness" factor... *"The Priest Fainted"* is one dish which tastes far too good to be healthy ... but it is! *Pissaladina* also takes a while to cook properly, but the result is far more mouthwatering than you could possibly believe from simply glancing at its list of ingredients.

So often in the Mediterranean it *is* the simplest dish which proves to be the best. I will never forget the first time I ate a plate of melted mozzarella with tomato at a friend's house in Italy. Even if I can't quite recreate at home the atmosphere of the bougainvillaea-covered terrace on which we lunched that day, the dish never fails to delight me and fill me full of the Mediterranean spirit—even on the grayest of days here at home.

OPPOSITE: Tunisian Eggs (page 72)

PISSALADINA
France

This deceptively simple dish is quite delicious and very easy to make.

Calories per serving: 382
Saturated fat: Low
Protein: Low
Carbohydrate: Low
Fiber: 10 g
Cholesterol: 4 mg
Vitamins: C, Folic acid, Niacin
Minerals: Iron, Potassium

1/3 cup olive oil
4 thick slices of whole-wheat bread, each weighing about 3 oz.
2 lb. onions, sliced
4 anchovy fillets
16 pitted ripe olives

Heat 2 tablespoons of the oil in a large pan and fry the slices of bread on one side only. Remove from the pan.

Add the remaining oil to the pan, reduce the heat as far as you can and very, very gently cook the onions until extremely soft–almost puréed. This will take up to an hour.

Preheat the oven to 375F (190C).

Spread the onion purée on the untoasted side of the bread slices. Put them on a baking sheet and bake 10 minutes. Garnish with anchovies and olives to serve.

MELTED MOZZARELLA & TOMATO
Italy

This is my favorite quick lunch dish, served with crusty bread to mop up the juices.

Calories per serving: 186
Saturated fat: High
Protein: High
Carbohydrate: Low
Fiber: 1.5 g
Cholesterol: 32 mg
Vitamins: Beta-carotene, C
Minerals: Calcium, Potassium

2 large ripe tomatoes, sliced
1/2 lb. Mozzarella cheese, thinly sliced
1-1/2 tbsp. olive oil
1-1/2 tsp. dried basil *or* 12 fresh basil leaves, chopped
Salt and pepper

In a shallow oval or oblong flameproof serving dish, arrange alternating slices of tomato and cheese in rows, so that half the cheese and half the tomato from each row is showing. Drizzle with the oil, sprinkle on the basil and season to taste.

Place the dish under a preheated broiler, or cook 30 seconds on HIGH in a microwave oven, until the cheese is just melting. Don't overcook or the cheese will become tough.

OPPOSITE: Pissaladina

"THE PRIEST FAINTED"
———— Turkey ————

The priest apparently passed out with pure pleasure when he tasted this dish – it is that good!

Calories per serving: 196
Saturated fat: Low
Protein: Low
Carbohydrate: Medium
Fiber: 9 g
Cholesterol: Nil
Vitamins: C, Folic acid, Beta-carotene
Minerals: Iron

2 large eggplants
1/4 cup olive oil
1 onion, finely chopped
1 large green bell pepper, seeded
1 (15-oz.) can tomatoes
1 garlic clove, chopped
1/3 cup raisins
1 tsp. brown sugar
Pinch of ground cinnamon
Salt and black pepper
1/2 cup tomato juice
1/4 cup chopped parsley, for garnish

Halve the eggplants and scoop out some of the flesh. Chop this and reserve it. Sprinkle some salt on the inside of the eggplant halves, turn them upside down on a plate, and let them drain about 30 minutes. This removes any bitterness. Rinse and pat dry.

Preheat the oven to 400F (205C). Heat 2 tablespoons of the oil in a large pan over medium heat and sauté the halves, cut-side down, for a few minutes. Transfer to a shallow ovenproof dish.

Add the remaining oil to the pan and sauté the onion until soft and lightly golden. Add the chopped eggplant and cook a few minutes longer, stirring. Add the green pepper and sauté briefly, then add the tomatoes, garlic, raisins, sugar, cinnamon, and seasoning to taste. Stir, and sauté a few minutes. Add some tomato juice if the mixture looks too dry. Fill the eggplant halves with the mixture.

Cover the bottom of the baking dish with tomato juice, arrange the stuffed eggplant halves on top, cover and bake 45 minutes, or until the eggplant flesh is soft right through when tested with a skewer.

Serve cool but not chilled, with the parsley sprinkled on top.

TUNISIAN EGGS
———— North Africa ————

Calories per serving: 170
Saturated fat: Medium
Protein: High
Carbohydrate: Low
Fiber: 2.5 g
Cholesterol: 250 mg
Vitamins: Beta-carotene, C, D, E
Minerals: Potassium, Iron

3 tbsp. olive oil
1 onion, sliced
2 small green bell peppers, seeded and sliced
2 small red bell peppers, seeded and sliced
2 large ripe tomatoes, sliced
1 tsp. ground cumin
Salt and black pepper
4 extra large eggs
Paprika, for garnish

Preheat the oven to 375F (190C).

Heat the oil in a skillet over medium heat and sauté the onion until soft. Add the sliced peppers and sauté a few more minutes, stirring frequently. Add the tomatoes and sauté 2 minutes longer. Add the cumin, and season.

Transfer the mixture to a shallow ovenproof dish or 4 individual gratin dishes. Make 4 indentations in the mixture and break an egg into each. Cover and bake 12 minutes, or until the eggs are just set. Garnish with the paprika and serve.

BAKED ZUCCHINI
—————— *Italy* ——————

This dish makes a filling supper, with some crusty bread and a tomato salad.

Calories per serving: 195
Saturated fat: High
Protein: High
Carbohydrate: Low
Fiber: 2 g
Cholesterol: 135 mg
Vitamins: Beta-carotene, C, D, E
Minerals: Iron, Calcium

1-1/2 lb. zucchini
Salt and black pepper
2 tbsp. safflower oil
1-1/2 tbsp. flour
1 tsp. dried marjoram
2 eggs, beaten
1/3 cup skim milk
1/2 cup grated Parmesan cheese
3 tbsp. bread crumbs

Slice the zucchini, sprinkle them with salt, and let them drain about 30 minutes. Rinse and pat dry.

Preheat the oven to 375F (190C).

Heat the oil in a skillet over medium heat. Dust the zucchini slices lightly with flour and fry them in the oil until tender and golden. Transfer to paper towels to drain, then arrange a layer of one-third of the zucchini slices on the bottom of a round ovenproof dish.

Sprinkle with one-fourth of the marjoram. Beat together the eggs, milk, half of the cheese, and salt and pepper to taste. Pour one-third of this over the zucchini. Cover with another layer of zucchini and marjoram, followed by another third of egg mixture. Repeat these layers once more. Top with the rest of the cheese and marjoram and the bread crumbs. Bake 30 minutes or until the egg is set throughout and the top is golden.

STUFFED EGGPLANT
—————— *Greece* ——————

This makes a filling hot supper, or you could serve it cold for lunch.

Calories per serving: 345
Saturated fat: Medium
Protein: High
Carbohydrate: Low
Fiber: 8.5 g
Cholesterol: 32 mg
Vitamins: B group, C,
   Beta-carotene, E
Minerals: Iron

2 large eggplants
Salt and black pepper
3 tbsp. olive oil
1 large onion, finely chopped
3/4 lb. very lean ground beef or
   lamb
1 (15-oz.) can tomatoes
1-1/2 cups cooked brown rice
2 tsp. ground cumin
2 tsp. ground coriander
A little meat stock
A little tomato juice
3 tbsp. chopped parsley, for garnish
3 tbsp. grated Parmesan cheese, for
   garnish

Halve the eggplants. Scoop out half of the flesh from each piece and chop it. Sprinkle the insides with salt and let them drain upside down 30 minutes. Rinse and pat dry.

Preheat the oven to 400F (205C).

Heat half of the oil in a skillet over medium heat and sauté the eggplant shells 2 minutes, turning frequently. Remove from the pan. Add the rest of the oil to the pan and sauté the onion until soft. Add the meat and brown thoroughly. Add the eggplant flesh, the tomatoes, rice, cumin, coriander and a little meat stock. Season well and simmer a few minutes.

Stuff the eggplant shells with the mixture. Place them in a shallow ovenproof dish with a little tomato juice on the bottom, cover and bake 1 hour, or until the eggplant is tender. Serve garnished with the parsley and Parmesan.

STUFFED BELL PEPPERS
——— Spain ———

This dish also makes a good first course, in which case the quantity here would serve eight people.

Calories per serving: 210
Saturated fat: Low
Protein: Low
Carbohydrate: Low
Fiber: 7.5 g
Cholesterol: Nil
Vitamins: Beta-carotene, C
Minerals: Iron

1-1/2 tbsp. olive oil
1 onion, finely chopped
1 garlic clove, minced
1 cup chopped mushrooms
1 large ripe tomato, chopped
1/4 cup cooked lentils *or* red kidney beans
1-1/2 tsp. tomato paste
1 tsp. dried basil
Pinch of chili powder
A little tomato juice
1 cup soft whole-wheat bread crumbs
Salt and black pepper
4 green bell peppers, halved lengthwise and seeded

Preheat the oven to 400F (205C).

Heat the oil in a skillet over medium heat and sauté the onion until soft and just turning golden. Add the garlic, mushrooms, tomato, lentils or beans, tomato paste, basil and chili powder. Cook 10 minutes longer, adding tomato juice as necessary to keep the mixture moist. Add the bread crumbs and stir 1 minute. Season.

Pile the mixture into the halved peppers and place them in a shallow ovenproof dish with a little tomato juice on the bottom. Cover and bake 1 hour, or until the peppers are tender. Serve hot or cold.

LAMB IN YOGURT SAUCE
——— Turkey ———

This is one of my favorite Mediterranean dishes and it is so easy to make.

Calories per serving: 475
Saturated fat: Medium
Protein: High
Carbohydrate: Low
Fiber: 3 g
Cholesterol: 135 mg
Vitamins: Niacin, E, Beta-carotene, C
Minerals: Iron, Potassium, Calcium

1-1/2 lb. lean boneless lamb
1 tbsp. butter
1/3 cup pine nuts
1-1/2 tbsp. olive oil
1 large ripe tomato, peeled and chopped
1 large garlic clove, chopped
Salt and black pepper
1 cup *Greek-Style Yogurt* (see page 124)
2 pita breads, preferably whole-wheat, halved

Cut the lamb into thin, bite-sized strips.

Heat the butter in a skillet over medium heat and sauté the pine nuts until golden. Remove from the pan and set aside. Add the olive oil to the pan and increase the heat. When it is really hot, add the lamb a few pieces at a time and brown them quickly. Remove the lamb and keep it warm.

Stir-fry the tomato and garlic in the remaining olive oil about 2 minutes, then transfer to a shallow serving dish. Season with salt and pepper and place the lamb on top. Add any meat juices to the yogurt and warm this a few seconds in the microwave oven, or in a small pan. Pour over the lamb. Scatter the pine nuts on the top. Keep warm while toasting the halved pitas. Serve the pitas to accompany the warm lamb mixture.

You can also serve this as a filling inside the pita bread, in which case it will fill 6 whole pitas, to serve 6.

OPPOSITE: Lamb in Yogurt Sauce

MUSSELS WITH TOMATO & BASIL SAUCE
France

Mussels are simple to prepare and cook, and are very low in fat.

Calories per serving: 143
Saturated fat: Low
Protein: High
Carbohydrate: Low
Fiber: 1.25 g
Cholesterol: 62 mg
Vitamins: C
Minerals: Iron, Potassium, Calcium

2 lb. fresh mussels in their shells
1 recipe *Tomato Sauce* (see page 101)
2 tbsp. chopped fresh basil

Scrub the mussels under cold running water and pull off their "beards." Discard any which are open and don't close when sharply tapped.

Make the tomato sauce, adding the extra chopped basil at the end of the cooking time.

Steam the mussels in a covered pan in a very little boiling water over high heat. In 1–2 minutes, the shells will begin to open. Transfer the opened mussels to a serving dish, discarding any which fail to open, pour on the sauce and serve.

FETA PITA POCKETS
Greece

Warmed filled pitas are the Mediterranean version of our sandwiches.

Calories per serving: 300
Saturated fat: Medium
Protein: Medium
Carbohydrate: High
Fiber: 6 g
Cholesterol: 25 mg
Vitamins: C, A
Minerals: Iron, Calcium

4 pita breads
4 oz. Greek Feta cheese
1 large ripe tomato, chopped
1 celery stalk, chopped
2-inch piece of cucumber, chopped
1/3 cup chopped green bell pepper
6 crisp lettuce leaves, shredded
1-1/2 tbsp. olive oil
A little lemon juice
1/2 tsp. dried basil
Black pepper

Warm the pitas in the oven. Meanwhile, crumble the cheese and combine it with the rest of the ingredients.

Fill the pitas with the mixture and serve.

TUNA PITA POCKETS
Greece

Calories per serving: 276
Saturated fat: Low
Protein: High
Carbohydrate: High
Fiber: 6.5 g
Cholesterol: 20 mg
Vitamins: Niacin, E, C
Minerals: Iron, Calcium

4 pita breads
1 (7-oz.) can tuna in oil, drained and flaked
1 large ripe tomato, chopped
1 small onion, finely chopped
2/3 cup canned cannellini beans, drained
2 tbsp. chopped parsley
1-1/2 tbsp. olive oil
1-1/2 tbsp. white wine vinegar
Black pepper

Warm the pitas in the oven. Meanwhile, combine the rest of the ingredients.

Fill the pitas with the tuna mixture and serve.

OPPOSITE: Mussels with Tomato & Basil Sauce

MAIN COURSES

Mediterranean meals often consist of simple grilled, baked or roasted fish, poultry or meat, served with salads and bread or potatoes.

However, there is also a rich variety of recipes, ranging from the quick and easy, to more time-consuming but not too difficult ones.

By no means all Mediterranean main course dishes are quick to prepare and cook. One of the dishes that, for me, most sums up traditional Mediterranean cooking is the delicious Greek *stiphado* of beef or rabbit which takes several hours of long, slow cooking in the oven to be at its most meltingly tender and succulent.

However, one of the reasons that I–an amateur cook and busy working mother–don't mind planning ahead to enjoy dishes such as this or, for instance, the *Moroccan Couscous*, is that the meals are unpretentious, the techniques are simple...and there is very little to go wrong. Although there is often much chopping and mixing involved, there is really nothing at all to *worry* about in the Mediterranean kitchen.

The recipes in this chapter reflect the relaxed attitude of the average Mediterranean cook– usually the housewife. There are dozens of different variations on these recipes, depending upon whose kitchen you are in at the time, so don't be afraid to experiment a little when you can.

Of course, many Mediterranean main courses need no recipe at all. What could be a better meal than a fresh, whole fish or a swordfish steak baked in a foil package with some chopped fresh herbs, lemon juice and black pepper?

Traditionally, meat was a rare commodity in the Mediterranean area. When available, it was stretched, as in the recipes in the following chapter. But pork chops, lamb kabobs and roasts cooked over an open fire are all part of the tradition of special occasions and should be enjoyed to the full every now and then without any feelings of guilt!

As most of the main course dishes are high in protein, they need a high-carbohydrate accompaniment, such as potatoes, rice or pasta, and salad or vegetables. If you are following one of the Plans in Chapters 3 or 4, you will find suitable suggestions for accompaniments there.

OPPOSITE: Honeyed Chicken (page 86)

RAISIN-BAKED SARDINES
—————— *Italy* ——————

Serve the sardines with a green salad and a few plain boiled potatoes.

Pine nuts make an excellent alternative to the almonds.

Calories per serving: 460
Saturated fat: Low
Protein: High
Carbohydrate: Low
Fiber: 1.5 g
Cholesterol: 170 mg
Vitamins: E, the B complex
Minerals: Iron, Calcium

12 large fresh sardines or small trout
10 blanched almonds
2 tbsp. soft whole-wheat bread crumbs
3 tbsp. golden raisins
1 lemon
Salt and black pepper
12 small bay leaves
1-1/2 tbsp. olive oil

Preheat the oven to 350F (175C).

Remove heads and tails from the sardines, then split them open. Remove their backbones and flatten the fish.

Chop the nuts and mix them with the bread crumbs, raisins and the juice of half of the lemon. Season to taste and spoon the mixture onto the flesh of 6 of the sardines. Place 2 bay leaves on each and top with the remaining sardines, skin-side up. Cut each lengthwise in half.

Pack the sardines closely in a shallow ovenproof dish. Sprinkle with the oil and bake about 30 minutes. Serve with the remaining lemon, cut into slices.

SWORDFISH STEAKS WITH ALMOND SAUCE
—————— *Spain* ——————

The Spanish love almonds, and this rich yet delicate sauce is one of the wonders of their cuisine. Serve the sauce cold to accompany grilled steaks.

Calories per serving: 438
Saturated fat: Low
Protein: High
Carbohydrate: Low
Fiber: 3 g
Cholesterol: 140 mg
Vitamins: E, C, Beta-carotene
Minerals: Iron, Calcium

1 small dried chile pepper
2/3 cup blanched almonds
1 cup canned tomatoes
1 tsp. paprika
1 garlic clove, chopped
Salt
1/3 cup olive oil
3 tbsp. red wine vinegar
4 swordfish steaks, each weighing about 6 oz.
A little tomato juice

Seed the chile pepper and soak it in a little water for a few minutes. Toast the almonds in a hot oven until golden, then grind them finely in a coffee mill.

Blend the tomatoes with the paprika, garlic and salt to taste in a food processor. Gradually blend in all but 1 tablespoon of the olive oil. Stir in the vinegar.

Brush the swordfish steaks with the reserved olive oil and cook them under the broiler.

Stir the almonds into the tomato sauce. If the sauce seems too thick, add a little tomato juice. Serve with the swordfish.

SHRIMP SKEWERS
—————— *Italy* ——————

Calories per serving: 180
Saturated fat: Low
Protein: High
Carbohydrate: Low
Fiber: Nil
Cholesterol: 215 mg
Vitamins: Niacin, Folic acid
Minerals: Calcium, Potassium

24 raw jumbo shrimp in their shells
3 tbsp. olive oil
3 tbsp. lemon juice
Salt and black pepper
Lemon wedges, to serve

Remove heads from the shrimp if it is necessary, but leave on their tails. Thread them onto 4 small skewers and place these in a shallow dish. Sprinkle with the oil, lemon juice, and a little salt and pepper. Let marinate 1 hour, turning a few times.

Grill the skewers a few minutes, basting with the juices from the dish. Serve with lemon wedges.

SPICY MONKFISH KABOBS
———— Greece ————

Monkfish is the perfect fish for kabobs as its firm, meaty flesh does not break up.

Calories per serving: 345
Saturated fat: Medium
Protein: High
Carbohydrate: Low
Fiber: 3 g
Cholesterol: 120 mg
Vitamins: C, Beta-carotene, Niacin
Minerals: Potassium

1 large green bell pepper
4 thick slices of bacon
1-1/2 lb. monkfish fillet, cubed
24 button mushrooms
8 bay leaves
For the sauce:
1 (15-oz.) can tomatoes
1-1/2 tbsp. tomato paste
1 large garlic clove, minced
3 tbsp. olive oil
1-1/2 tbsp. honey
3 tbsp. red wine vinegar
1 tsp. chili sauce
1-1/2 tbsp. soy sauce
1-1/2 tsp. dried oregano

To make the sauce, heat the ingredients together in a saucepan, stirring thoroughly. Let simmer gently while preparing the kabobs.

Seed the pepper and cut it into squares. Cut the bacon into squares.

Using 4 long skewers or 8 short ones, arrange the fish, mushrooms, squares of pepper and bacon and the bay leaves on the skewers. Brush with a little sauce and broil about 10 minutes, turning at least once and basting, until the fish is golden and the peppers slightly charred.

Add the juices from the broiler pan to the sauce and stir. Serve with the kabobs.

SCALLOPS WITH MUSHROOMS
———— France ————

Calories per serving: 220
Saturated fat: Low
Protein: High
Carbohydrate: Low
Fiber: 1.5 g
Cholesterol: 48 mg
Vitamins: C
Minerals: Iron, Potassium

3 tbsp. olive oil
1-1/4 lb. fresh shelled scallops, cut horizontally in half
3 garlic cloves, minced
24 button mushrooms, halved
1/3 cup full-bodied dry white wine
1/3 cup chopped parsley
Salt and black pepper

Heat the oil in a skillet over medium heat, add the scallops and sauté them 2–3 minutes only–scallops are ruined if overcooked!

Add the garlic and mushrooms and stir 30 seconds only, then add the wine, parsley and seasoning. Simmer gently a few seconds and serve.

SQUID IN RED WINE
———— Spain ————

Squid is best purchased ready-prepared.

Calories per serving: 370
Saturated fat: Low
Protein: High
Carbohydrate: Low
Fiber: 1.5 g
Cholesterol: 120 mg
Vitamins: Niacin, B12, A, C
Minerals: Iron, Potassium

3 tbsp. olive oil
1 large onion, thinly sliced
2 garlic cloves, chopped
Squid, weighing about 2-1/4 lb., cleaned and cut into strips
2 large ripe tomatoes, peeled and chopped
1 tsp. dried oregano
1 bay leaf
1 tbsp. tomato paste
Salt and black pepper
2/3 cup red wine
1-1/2 tsp. cornstarch

Heat the oil in a skillet which has a lid and sauté the onion, uncovered, until translucent and just turning golden. Add the garlic and squid slices and sauté a few minutes only.

Add the tomatoes, herbs, tomato paste and seasoning, stir and cook 1 minute. Add the wine and simmer 2 minutes.

Mix the cornstarch with a very little cold water and add to the pan. Stir, then cover and simmer very gently about 45 minutes or until the squid is tender and the sauce is thickened.

OVERLEAF: Shrimp Skewers and Swordfish Steaks with Almond Sauce

SHRIMP PROVENÇAL
—————— *France* ——————

Calories per serving: 203
Saturated fat: Low
Protein: High
Carbohydrate: Low
Fiber: 1.5 g
Cholesterol: 162 mg
Vitamins: C, Beta-carotene
Minerals: Calcium, Potassium

3 tbsp. olive oil
1 onion, finely chopped
2 garlic cloves, chopped
1 (15-oz) can tomatoes
3/4 cup dry white wine
1 small chile pepper, seeded and
    chopped
1 bay leaf
Black pepper
3/4 lb. peeled cooked shrimp
3 tbsp. chopped parsley, for garnish

Heat the oil in a skillet over medium heat and sauté the onion in it until soft and just turning golden. Add the garlic and stir a few seconds. Add the tomatoes, wine, chile pepper, bay leaf and pepper to taste. Simmer about 30 minutes, until it becomes a rich sauce.

Just before serving, add the shrimp and simmer gently a few minutes only. Sprinkle with the parsley and serve.

BAKED SEA BASS
—————— *Greece* ——————

If sea bass is not available, use swordfish, cod or halibut.

Calories per serving: 425
Saturated fat: Low
Protein: High
Carbohydrate: Low
Fiber: 3.5 g
Cholesterol: 150 mg
Vitamins: Beta-carotene, C
Minerals: Calcium, Potassium

3 tbsp. olive oil
1 large onion, sliced
2 carrots, sliced
2 celery stalks, chopped
1 large garlic clove, minced
2 large ripe tomatoes, peeled and
    chopped
1/4 cup dry white wine
4 sea bass steaks, each weighing
    about 8 oz.
Salt and black pepper

Preheat the oven to 350F (175C).

Heat the oil in a skillet and sauté the onion until translucent. Add the carrots and celery and stir a few minutes. Add the garlic and a small wineglass of water, then season. Cover and simmer 10 minutes. Add the tomatoes and simmer a few minutes longer, then add the wine. Simmer gently a few seconds.

Put the fish in an oiled baking dish, cover with sauce and bake 30 minutes.

SARDINIAN SEAFOOD STEW
—————— *Sardinia* ——————

The fish and seafood can vary according to availability: my favorite mix is red mullet, porgy and pollock with scallops, shrimp, and squid cut into strips.

Calories per serving: 490
Saturated fat: Low
Protein: High
Carbohydrate: Low
Fiber: 3 g
Cholesterol: 227 mg
Vitamins: Beta-carotene, C, E
Minerals: Iron, Calcium

1/3 cup olive oil
2 onions, finely chopped
1 leek, finely chopped
4 garlic cloves
4 canned tomatoes, seeded
1 tsp. dried fennel
1 large bay leaf
Large pinch of saffron
Piece of orange zest
1 quart fish stock
Salt and black pepper
4 lb. assorted fish (see left), cut
    into chunks
1-1/2 lb. assorted seafood (see left)
3 tbsp. chopped parsley

Heat the oil in a Dutch oven over medium heat. Sauté the onions and leek in it until they are soft and just golden. Add the garlic and tomatoes and simmer 2 minutes. Add the herbs, saffron, orange zest and stock, season and bring to a boil. Beat to emulsify.

Reduce the heat and add any firm-fleshed fish, such as mullet and porgy. Simmer 5 minutes, then add the seafood and any soft-fleshed fish, such as pollock. Simmer 3 minutes longer.

Immediately transfer the seafood and fish to a serving dish. Pour on some of the vegetables and liquid and sprinkle with the chopped parsley.

CHICKEN WITH 30 CLOVES OF GARLIC
——— *France* ———

If garlic cloves are thoroughly cooked they become mellow and deliciously nutty.

Calories per serving: 400
Saturated fat: Medium
Protein: High
Carbohydrate: Low
Fiber: 1 g
Cholesterol: 180 mg
Vitamins: Niacin, Folic acid, C
Minerals: Iron, Potassium

1 small roasting chicken
30 large cloves of garlic, unpeeled
2 tsp. garlic paste (optional)
Juice of 1 lemon, plus 1/4 lemon
Salt and black pepper
4 sprigs of fresh thyme *or* 1 tsp.
   dried thyme
1 tbsp. butter
1-1/2 tbsp. olive oil

Preheat the oven to 400F (205C).

Put the chicken on a piece of foil large enough to wrap around it. Arrange the garlic cloves on either side. Put some of the garlic paste, if using, and a wedge of lemon inside the bird with some salt and pepper. Spread any remaining garlic paste on the breast of the chicken and sprinkle with the thyme and a little more salt and pepper. Dot the butter on the breast and finally pour on the olive oil and lemon juice. Fold the foil together along the top of the chicken to make a loose package.

Roast 1-1/4 hours, then open the foil and return to the oven to let the chicken brown, about 15 minutes.

Serve the chicken with the whole garlic cloves and the cooking juices.

HONEYED CHICKEN
——— *Spain* ———

For even less calories, remove the skin from the chicken breasts.

Calories per serving: 370
Saturated fat: Medium
Protein: High
Carbohydrate: Low
Fiber: Trace
Cholesterol: 100 mg
Vitamins: Niacin, C
Minerals: Iron

4 chicken breast halves
Salt and black pepper
3 tbsp. olive oil
1 onion, finely chopped
Grated zest of 1 lemon
1/4 cup honey
1 tsp. dried rosemary *or* 1 sprig of
   fresh rosemary, chopped
3/4 cup dry white wine
6 anchovy fillets, rinsed

Preheat the oven to 325F (165C).

Season the chicken portions with salt and pepper. Heat the oil in a skillet and sauté the chicken until golden. Transfer to a casserole dish.

Sauté the onion in the skillet until soft and add that to the casserole.

Combine the lemon zest, honey and rosemary in a small pan and warm through. Pour this mixture over the contents of the casserole and bake 30 minutes.

At the end of this time, add the wine and anchovies and return to the oven to bake 15 minutes longer, or until the chicken is tender.

CHICKEN WITH PINE NUTS
——— Spain ———

Calories per serving: 425
Saturated fat: Low
Protein: High
Carbohydrate: Low
Fiber: 3 g
Cholesterol: 112 mg
Vitamins: Beta-carotene, C, E
Minerals: Iron, Potassium

3 tbsp. olive oil
4 skinless, boneless chicken breast
   halves, each cut into 4
1 onion, finely chopped
1 red bell pepper, seeded and
   chopped
1 garlic clove, chopped
1-1/2 tsp. flour
Salt and black pepper
1-1/2 tbsp. chopped parsley
1/3 cup pine nuts
1/2 cup dry Spanish sherry

Heat the oil in a skillet over high heat and sauté the chicken 1 minute to brown each side. Remove and keep warm.

Sauté the onion until soft, then add the bell pepper and sauté a few minutes longer. Add the garlic, stir and add the flour, salt and pepper. Stir again, then add the parsley, pine nuts, chicken and sherry.

Simmer 10 minutes, or until the chicken is cooked through, adding a little water or chicken stock if the dish looks too dry.

SOUVLAKIA
——— Greece ———

Often the simplest dishes taste the best, and this is simply delicious.

Calories per serving: 390
Saturated fat: Medium
Protein: High
Carbohydrate: Low
Fiber: Trace
Cholesterol: 128 mg
Vitamins: Niacin, B12
Minerals: Iron, Potassium

1-1/2 lb. lean boneless lamb, cut
   into small cubes
16 bay leaves
1/4 cup olive oil
3 tbsp. lemon juice
2 tsp. dried oregano
Salt and black pepper
1 lemon, cut into wedges, to serve

Soak 8 small wooden skewers well in water. Thread the lamb onto the skewers, with a bay leaf at either end of each.

Lay the skewers in a shallow dish and drizzle with the oil and lemon juice. Sprinkle on the oregano, salt and pepper and let marinate 1–2 hours, turning from time to time.

Grill or broil the skewers, basting once or twice, and serve with lemon wedges.

The skewers go well with *Tzatziki* (page 58) and a plain tomato and onion salad.

ROAST LAMB
——— Greece ———

In Greece, the lamb is roasted very slowly for hours, until it virtually falls off the bone.

Calories per serving: 460
Saturated fat: Medium
Protein: High
Carbohydrate: Low
Fiber: Nil
Cholesterol: 128 mg
Vitamins: Niacin, B12
Minerals: Iron, Potassium

1/3 cup olive oil
3 tbsp. honey
1-1/2 tbsp. crushed dried rosemary
2 garlic cloves, minced
4 thick lamb steaks, cut from the
   leg

Preheat the oven to 325F (165C).

Mix the oil, honey, rosemary and garlic thoroughly in a small bowl and coat the lamb steaks with the mixture.

Put the steaks in a roasting pan and roast 2 hours, basting from time to time, until the lamb is a rich, dark color and falls easily from the bone.

If you have the time you can roast at a lower temperature for a longer time, for even better results.

LAMB IN WHITE WINE
—————— Greece ——————

This tastes even better if kept overnight and reheated the next day.

Calories per serving: 375
Saturated fat: Medium
Protein: High
Carbohydrate: Low
Fiber: 0.5 g
Cholesterol: 128 mg
Vitamins: Niacin, B12,
*   Beta-carotene*
Minerals: Iron, Potassium

3 tbsp. olive oil
1-1/2 lb. lean boneless lamb, cubed
1 garlic clove, finely chopped
1/3 cup dry white wine
3 tbsp. lemon juice
1 cup canned tomatoes
1-1/2 tbsp. chopped parsley
Salt and black pepper

Heat the oil in a skillet over high heat and sauté the lamb a little at a time until uniformly brown. Remove the lamb.

Reduce the heat and add the garlic. Sauté briefly. Return the lamb to the pan and add the wine, lemon juice, tomatoes and parsley. Season and simmer 10 minutes, adding a little water if necessary.

LAMB & APRICOT CASSEROLE
—————— Morocco ——————

Try replacing half of the apricots with chopped dates or golden raisins for a different flavor.

Calories per serving: 450
Saturated fat: Medium
Protein: High
Carbohydrate: Low
Fiber: 9 g
Cholesterol: 130 mg
Vitamins: Niacin, B12, C,
*   Beta-carotene*
Minerals: Iron, Potassium

1-1/2 tbsp. olive oil
1-1/2 lb. lean boneless lamb, cubed
1 large onion, chopped
1 large green bell pepper, seeded
    and sliced
1 tbsp. flour
2/3 cup canned chickpeas
Large pinch of saffron
Salt and black pepper
1 tsp. ground allspice
About 2 cups good meat stock
1 cup dried apricots
1-1/2 tbsp. lemon juice

Preheat the oven to 350F (175C).

Heat the oil in a Dutch oven over high heat and brown the lamb a few cubes at a time. Remove the lamb.

Add the onion and bell pepper to the pan and sauté them until soft. Return the meat to the pan. Add the flour, stir and add the chickpeas, saffron, salt, pepper and allspice along with just enough stock to cover the meat.

Cover and bake 1 hour, then add the apricots and lemon juice. Add a little more stock if the sauce is looking too dry. Return the pan to the oven to bake 15 minutes longer. Adjust the seasoning, if necessary, before serving.

OPPOSITE: Lamb & Apricot Casserole

PORK TENDERLOIN MARSALA
——— *Italy* ———

The traditional recipe does not contain the yogurt, but I find it makes a much nicer sauce.

Calories per serving: 275
Saturated fat: High
Protein: High
Carbohydrate: Low
Fiber: Nil
Cholesterol: 110 mg
Vitamins: B group
Minerals: Potassium, Iron

4 pork tenderloins, each weighing about 6 oz.
3 tbsp. corn oil
1/4 cup Marsala wine
Salt and black pepper
3 tbsp. *Greek-Style Yogurt* (see page 124)

Slice each tenderloin of pork into 3 or 4 medallions. Heat the oil in a skillet over high heat and brown the medallions about 1 minute on each side.

Add the Marsala, season with salt and pepper and boil briefly. Reduce the heat and simmer a few minutes, until the pork is cooked through.

Transfer the pork to serving plates. Stir the yogurt into the pan juices, adjust the seasoning and pour over the pork to serve.

PORK WITH ORANGES
——— *Spain* ———

Calories per serving: 256
Saturated fat: High
Protein: High
Carbohydrate: Low
Fiber: Trace
Cholesterol: 110 mg
Vitamins: B group, C
Minerals: Potassium, Iron

1-1/2 tbsp. olive oil
4 pork tenderloins, each weighing about 6 oz.
1/2 cup dry sherry
Grated zest of 2 oranges
3 tbsp. orange juice
1/4 cup chicken stock
1/2 tsp. ground ginger
Salt and black pepper

Heat the oil in a skillet over high heat and brown the pork tenderloins about 1 minute on each side.

Add the sherry and bring to a boil. Reduce the heat and add the rest of the ingredients. Season well and simmer, covered, about 20 minutes.

RABBIT STIPHADO
——— *Greece* ———

You can use lean beef instead of the rabbit, in which case there will be 350 calories and 84 mg cholesterol per serving.

Calories per serving: 280
Saturated fat: Medium
Protein: High
Carbohydrate: Low
Fiber: 3 g
Cholesterol: 70 mg
Vitamins: B12, Niacin, C, Beta-carotene
Minerals: Iron, Potassium

1 large rabbit or 2 small rabbits, cut into pieces (or 1-1/4 lb. flank steak)
1-1/2 lb. small onions, peeled but left whole
1 (15-oz.) can tomatoes
3 garlic cloves, minced
2 bay leaves
Salt and black pepper
For the marinade:
1-3/4 cups hearty red wine
1/3 cup red wine vinegar
3 tbsp. olive oil
A few black peppercorns
1 tsp. whole allspice

Mix together the marinade ingredients in an casserole dish and add the rabbit pieces. Cover and let marinate in the refrigerator several hours or overnight.

Preheat the oven to 325F (165C).

Pour off a little of the marinade and reserve. Add the onions, tomatoes, garlic, bay leaves and seasoning to the casserole. Pour back just enough of the marinade barely to cover the meat. Cover and cook in the oven 5 hours.

OPPOSITE: Pork with Oranges

90

PASTA & GRAINS

Pasta and grains are the basis of many Mediterranean dishes. Together they supply a high percentage of the carbohydrates that make up a large part of a healthy diet. No one need feel guilty about indulging in a plate of steaming spaghetti or a spiced rice dish.

Pasta has a totally unfair reputation outside of Italy for being fattening. This is probably because in the typical *trattoria* in this country you will find pasta dishes which are laden with cream, butter, cheese and meat.

However, this is not how pasta is traditionally eaten. Even today, in Southern Italy, you will find a big pot of boiled pasta served for the family with only a little tomato sauce or, even simpler, with a trickle of olive oil, some black pepper, and a sprinkling of grated Parmesan—a cheese which goes a very long way! With a dinner salad, this is a perfect meal all year round.

The pasta sauces in this chapter vary from light to rich-tasting. However, the richness comes from the flavorful Mediterranean vegetables, nuts, and so on that I have used rather than from any high-saturated-fat additions.

Whole-wheat pasta can be used in any of the recipes, but I must confess that I prefer the hard durum wheat pasta, so beloved by the Italians themselves. It contains slightly less fiber than whole-wheat pasta, but the difference really is not enough to worry about.

For the grain dishes, I have given my own versions of the classics: the wonderful paellas, risottos and pilafs of the Mediterranean which are very familiar to us all. North African *Couscous* is less well-known; the light, almost fluffy couscous grain with its accompanying stew makes a marvelous dinner party meal which is easily adapted if you are serving large numbers.

Plain boiled rice or pasta can be served instead of bread or potatoes with any meal. Rice can be enlivened by adding saffron or turmeric, chopped herbs or tiny pieces of fruit or vegetables for added color, taste and texture. Pasta needs nothing other than cooking until it is just *al dente*, and remember always to add a little oil to the cooking water to prevent the pasta sticking together.

OPPOSITE: Couscous (page 95)

TOMATO & MUSHROOM RISOTTO
—————— *Italy* ——————

Risottos are remarkably adaptable and this is a simple one to get you started.

Calories per serving: 440
Saturated fat: Low
Protein: Medium
Carbohydrate: High
Fiber: 5.5 g
Cholesterol: 9 mg
Vitamins: C, Beta-carotene
Minerals: Potassium, Calcium

1 (15-oz.) can tomatoes, chopped
1-1/2 tbsp. tomato paste
1/4 cup olive oil
1 onion, finely chopped
1 garlic clove, chopped
3/4 lb. mushrooms
1-1/4 cups Arborio rice
About 3-1/2 cups vegetable stock
Salt and black pepper
5 chopped fresh basil leaves *or*
   1 tsp. dried basil
3 tbsp. chopped parsley
3/4 cup grated Parmesan cheese, to
   serve

Mix the tomatoes with the tomato paste in a bowl. Heat the oil in a large skillet over medium heat and sauté the onion until soft and just turning golden. Add the garlic and stir 30 seconds. Add the mushrooms and stir again. Add the rice, stir and then pour in the tomatoes with half of the stock. Season and add the herbs.

Bring to a boil, then lower the heat and simmer gently. As the liquid is absorbed, add a little more. Continue simmering up to 45 minutes, adding more stock as necessary, until the rice is creamy, moist and tender. Serve sprinkled with the cheese.

LAMB PILAF
—————— *Turkey* ——————

I have used risotto rice for this recipe, but you could use long-grain white or brown rice.

Calories per serving: 575
Saturated fat: Low
Protein: High
Carbohydrate: Medium
Fiber: 6 g
Cholesterol: 64 mg
Vitamins: Niacin, B12, E, C
Minerals: Iron, Potassium, Calcium

3 tbsp. corn oil
1 large onion, finely chopped
3/4 lb. lean boneless lamb, cut into
   small pieces
2-1/4 cups Arborio rice
1 small eggplant, chopped
About 3-1/2 cups chicken stock
1 large ripe tomato, seeded and
   chopped
3 tbsp. currants
3 tbsp. raisins
3 tbsp. pine nuts
1-1/2 tbsp. blanched almonds,
   chopped
1 garlic clove, chopped
1 tsp. ground allspice
Salt and pepper

Heat the oil in a large skillet over medium heat and sauté the onion until soft and translucent. Add the lamb and stir 1 minute. Add the rice and stir well, then add the eggplant and stir again. Add half of the stock and the remaining ingredients and simmer until the rice is tender and creamy and has absorbed all the liquid, adding the rest of the stock as necessary during the cooking.

COUSCOUS
——— Morocco ———

Virtually all couscous available in this country is pre-cooked and easy to prepare.

This serves 4 very hungry people and could easily serve 6 as part of a three-course meal, in which case it would be 460 calories per serving.

You can use a whole cut-up chicken for the couscous instead of breast halves and make a chicken stock with the carcass to use instead of water in this recipe.

Calories per serving: 690
Saturated fat: Low
Protein: High
Carbohydrate: Medium
Fiber: 7 g
Cholesterol: 87 mg
Vitamins: Beta-carotene, Niacin, C, A, E
Minerals: Iron, Potassium

1/4 cup olive oil
4 chicken breast halves, skinned
2 onions, quartered
2 carrots, quartered
4 small turnips, trimmed
1-1/2 tbsp. tomato paste
1 large ripe tomato, chopped
2/3 cup canned chickpeas
1 large garlic clove, chopped
1 tsp. turmeric
1 tsp. ground coriander
1 tsp. ground cumin
Salt and black pepper
1-2/3 cups quick-cooking couscous
1 tbsp. butter
2 tbsp. toasted almonds, for garnish
2 tbsp. raisins, for garnish
3 tbsp. chopped parsley, for garnish

Heat 1 tablespoon of the oil in a large Dutch oven over medium heat and sauté the chicken about 1 minute until slightly golden. Add water to cover and bring to a boil, skimming off any froth that appears on the top. Add the onions, carrots, turnips, tomato paste, tomato, half of the chickpeas, the garlic, turmeric, coriander, cumin, seasoning, and enough extra water barely to cover the vegetables. Simmer 20 minutes.

Meanwhile, soak the couscous in a bowl of water 20 minutes, then drain and put in a saucepan with 2 tablespoons of water and the rest of the chickpeas. Heat gently, stirring frequently.

When the meat and vegetables are ready, stir the butter into the couscous, along with the remaining olive oil and a few tablespoons of the vegetable broth. Pile it on a serving plate and make a well in the center.

Using a slotted spoon, transfer the chicken from the pan and arrange it in the well in the center of the couscous. Garnish with the almonds, raisins and parsley and serve the broth and vegetables in a separate bowl for guests to help themselves.

RICE WITH BELL PEPPERS & PORK
——— Spain ———

This is similar to a risotto, but traditional risottos never use long-grain rice or saffron.

Calories per serving: 396
Saturated fat: Low
Protein: High
Carbohydrate: High
Fiber: 3 g
Cholesterol: 55 mg
Vitamins: Niacin, B12, Beta-carotene, C
Minerals: Potassium, Iron

1-1/2 tbsp. olive oil
3/4 lb. pork tenderloin, cut into small cubes
1 onion, finely chopped
3 garlic cloves, chopped
1 red and 1 yellow or green bell pepper, seeded and chopped
1 cup canned tomatoes
1-1/2 tbsp. chopped parsley
Salt and black pepper
Large pinch of saffron
1-2/3 cups long-grain rice
2-1/2 cups vegetable stock

Heat the oil in a Dutch oven over high heat and brown the pork a little at a time. Remove the pork.

Reduce the heat, add the onion and sauté it until translucent. Return the meat to the pan, add the garlic and stir 30 seconds. Add the bell peppers, tomatoes, parsley, seasoning and saffron and simmer 20 minutes.

Add the rice and stock, stir and bring to a boil, then reduce the heat and simmer 20 minutes, or until most of the liquid is absorbed and the rice is tender.

PAELLA
———— Spain ————

For the paella to be authentic, you really do need to use some fresh shellfish and at least some of the shrimp should have their tails left on. The whole point of paella is the lovely saffron flavor, so use the best.

Calories per serving: 685
Saturated fat: Low
Protein: High
Carbohydrate: Low
Fiber: 8 g
Cholesterol: 278 mg
Vitamins: Beta-carotene, Niacin, C, E
Minerals: Calcium, Potassium, Iron

20 fresh mussels in their shells (or 5 oz. shelled frozen mussels, thawed)
4 small boneless chicken breast halves
1 small tomato
1 red bell pepper
1 green bell pepper
1/2 tsp. saffron strands
3 tbsp. olive oil
1 small onion, very finely chopped
1 tsp. paprika
Salt and black pepper
3-1/2 cups chicken stock
1-2/3 cups long-grain rice
3/4 cup cooked green peas
8 raw jumbo shrimp, with tails on
1/2 lb. peeled cooked small shrimp

Scrub fresh mussels and remove their beards. Discard any that don't close when you tap them sharply.

Skin the chicken breasts and cut each into 4. Seed and chop the tomato and bell peppers. Soak the saffron strands in a little water.

Heat the oil in a large skillet or paella pan over medium heat and sauté the chicken pieces 1–2 minutes until golden. Add the tomato, bell peppers, onion, saffron, paprika and seasoning together with a little stock and simmer 15 minutes.

Add the rice, peas, jumbo shrimp and more stock. Simmer until the rice is tender, adding more stock as needed.

Stir in the small shrimp, then add the mussels. When they open, the paella is ready.

VEGETABLE LASAGNE
———— Italy ————

The lasagne can be varied by using sliced mushrooms in place of the zucchini.

Calories per serving: 400
Saturated fat: Low
Protein: High
Carbohydrate: Low
Fiber: 8 g
Cholesterol: 133 mg
Vitamins: Beta-carotene, A, C, E
Minerals: Iron, Calcium

1 small eggplant, sliced
1/2 lb. zucchini, sliced
1/2 cup brown lentils, washed
3 tbsp. olive oil
1 onion, chopped
1 (15-oz.) can tomatoes
1 large green bell pepper, seeded and chopped
1 tsp. dried oregano
Salt and black pepper
1 cup vegetable stock
8 sheets cooked lasagne verdi
2 eggs
1/3 cup skim milk
1-1/4 cups *Greek-Style Yogurt* (see page 124)
1/3 cup grated Parmesan cheese

Put the eggplant and zucchini in a colander and sprinkle with salt. Let drain 30 minutes. Rinse and pat dry. Cook the lentils in boiling water about 1 hour, until tender.

Preheat the oven to 375F (190C).

Heat the oil in a skillet over medium heat and sauté the onion a few minutes until soft. Add the zucchini and eggplant and stir-fry a few minutes. Add the tomatoes, bell pepper, drained lentils, oregano, seasoning and a little stock. Cover and simmer 20 minutes. Add more stock as needed to make the sauce the right consistency.

In a suitable ovenproof dish, spread a layer of half of the vegetable sauce followed by 4 sheets of lasagne, then more sauce and the remaining lasagne.

Beat together the eggs and milk in a bowl, then stir in the yogurt. Pour evenly on the lasagne and sprinkle the cheese on top. Bake 40 minutes.

OPPOSITE: Paella

RICOTTA & EGGPLANT SAUCE
———— *Italy* ————

This sauce combines well with pasta shells or spaghetti.

Calories per serving: 196
Saturated fat: Low
Protein: Low
Carbohydrate: Low
Fiber: 4 g
Cholesterol: 9 mg
Vitamins: Beta-carotene, C
Minerals: Iron, Calcium

1 eggplant, chopped
Salt
3 tbsp. olive oil
1 recipe *Tomato Sauce* (see page 101)
1/2 cup Ricotta cheese

Sprinkle the chopped eggplant with salt and let drain 30 minutes in a colander. Rinse and pat dry.

Heat the oil in a skillet over medium heat and sauté the eggplant, stirring, until fairly soft. Add the tomato sauce and simmer 30 minutes.

Just before serving, add the cheese to the sauce.

MUSHROOM SAUCE
———— *Italy* ————

Mushroom sauce is a perfect accompaniment to fettuccine or tagliatelle.

Calories per serving: 85
Saturated fat: Low
Protein: Low
Carbohydrate: Low
Fiber: 1.5 g
Cholesterol: 1 mg
Vitamins: B3, C
Minerals: Potassium, Calcium

3 tbsp. olive oil
2 garlic cloves, finely chopped
1/2 lb. mushrooms, chopped
2/3 cup *Greek-Style Yogurt* (see page 124)
Salt and pepper
3 tbsp. chopped parsley, for garnish

Heat the oil in a skillet over medium heat and sauté the garlic 30 seconds, stirring. Add the mushrooms and stir-fry 5 minutes. Add the yogurt and seasoning and warm through.

Pour onto the cooked and drained pasta and garnish with the parsley.

WALNUT SAUCE
———— *Italy* ————

Calories per serving: 293
Saturated fat: Medium
Protein: Medium
Carbohydrate: Low
Fiber: 2.25 g
Cholesterol: 6 mg
Vitamins: E, B group
Minerals: Calcium, Iron, Potassium

1-1/4 cups *Greek-Style Yogurt* (see page 124)
1 tsp. yeast extract
1-1/2 cups finely chopped walnuts
Salt and black pepper
1/3 cup grated Parmesan cheese, to serve
3 tbsp. chopped parsley, for garnish

Mix the yogurt with the yeast extract and heat gently in a small saucepan. Stir in the nuts and seasoning.

Pour onto the cooked and drained pasta and sprinkle with the cheese and some black pepper. Garnish with the parsley.

LENTIL SAUCE
Italy

Calories per serving: 265
Saturated fat: Low
Protein: High
Carbohydrate: High
Fiber: 9.5 g
Cholesterol: Nil
Vitamins: C, Beta-carotene
Minerals: Iron

1-1/2 tbsp. olive oil
1 onion, finely chopped
1 garlic clove, finely chopped
1 leek, sliced
1-1/2 cups green or brown lentils
1 large carrot, cut into 4
1 bay leaf
3-1/2 cups light vegetable stock or
    water
Salt and black pepper

Heat the oil in a heavy saucepan over medium heat and sauté the onion until soft and translucent. Add the garlic and stir. Add the leek and cook 2 minutes longer, stirring. Add the lentils, carrot, bay leaf and stock and simmer 1 hour, or until the lentils are tender, adding extra liquid if necessary. Remove the carrot and bay leaf.

Purée two-thirds of the lentils in a blender and return to the remaining contents of the pan; stir. Check the seasoning, and add salt if necessary.

CHILE-BELL PEPPER SAUCE
Spain

This piquant sauce goes well with pasta, but is also excellent with grilled fish.

Calories per serving: 50
Saturated fat: Low
Protein: Medium
Carbohydrate: High
Fiber: 1 g
Cholesterol: 1 mg
Vitamins: Beta-carotene, C
Minerals: Potassium

2 small, fresh chile peppers
2 large red bell peppers, seeded and
    chopped
2 tsp. sugar
3 tbsp. vinegar
6 canned anchovy fillets, drained

Slit the chile peppers and seed them. Chop them as finely as you can, then put them in a blender with the rest of the ingredients and purée to make a smooth sauce. Serve gently warmed or at room temperature.

PESTO
Italy

Pesto is very rich. Once made it will keep in the refrigerator 1–2 weeks.

Calories per serving: 270
Saturated fat: Medium
Protein: Medium
Carbohydrate: Low
Fiber: 0.5 g
Cholesterol: 9 mg
Vitamins: E, C
Minerals: Calcium

1 large garlic clove
2 cups chopped fresh basil leaves
Salt and black pepper
3 tbsp. pine nuts
1/2 cup grated Parmesan cheese
1/2 cup olive oil

Using a pestle and mortar, crush the garlic. Add the basil and pound to a paste with a little salt. Add the pine nuts and pound again, then repeat with the cheese.

Drizzle in the oil, a little at a time, and continue pounding until you have a thick sauce. Add salt and pepper to taste.

Pesto goes well with all kinds of pasta and is also nice stirred into minestrone. You can warm it gently to serve it, but do not bring it to a boil.

OLIVE OIL & GARLIC SAUCE
—————— *Spain* ——————

This is a less rich version of the French aïoli, *which includes eggs.*

Calories for the total batch: 1570 (serves 4–10 people)
Saturated fat: Medium
Protein: Trace
Carbohydrate: Trace
Fiber: 1 g
Cholesterol: Nil
Vitamins: Trace
Minerals: Trace

8 large garlic cloves
1 tsp. salt
3/4 cup extra-virgin olive oil

Using a pestle and mortar, pound the garlic and salt until well blended. Add the oil drop by drop, pounding until it has a smooth consistency.

This sauce is good with all grilled foods and can also be used as a dip with crusty bread.

TOMATO SAUCE
—————— *Italy* ——————

Always have a batch of tomato sauce on hand, as it can be used in so many ways.

Calories per serving: 87
Saturated fat: Medium
Protein: Low
Carbohydrate: Low
Fiber: 1.5 g
Cholesterol: Nil
Vitamins: C, Beta-carotene
Minerals: Potassium

3 tbsp. olive oil
1 onion, very finely chopped
1 garlic clove, chopped
1 (15-oz.) can tomatoes *or* 1 lb. ripe fresh tomatoes, peeled
1 tbsp. chopped parsley
1/2 tsp. sugar
1-1/2 tbsp. tomato paste
1 tsp. lemon juice
1 bay leaf
Salt and black pepper
1 tbsp. chopped fresh basil
A little tomato juice, as necessary

Heat the oil in a skillet over medium heat and sauté the onion until very soft – this may take 20 minutes or more. Add the garlic and stir. Add the remaining ingredients except the basil and tomato juice and simmer 20–30 minutes to make a rich sauce.

Remove the bay leaf and add the basil. Stir and season to taste. If the sauce has become too thick you can thin it with a little tomato juice.

I prefer the sauce made with canned tomatoes, unless the fresh tomatoes are really ripe and tasty.

Variations: Add 1 teaspoon of hot pepper sauce or chili powder to taste for a spicier sauce (this adds no calories); add 2/3 cup chopped mushrooms for the last 5 minutes of cooking (adds 2 calories per portion); add 1 small chopped red bell pepper with the tomatoes (adds 4 calories per portion).

OPPOSITE: Chile-Bell Pepper Sauce (page 99); Pesto (page 99); rigatoni with Ricotta & Eggplant Sauce (page 98)

SALADS & VEGETABLES

No Mediterranean cook would feel happy without a regular supply of seasonal salad greens and vegetables. In this chapter you will see how to create tempting main-course salads and vegetable and salad side dishes from the widest possible array of health-giving produce.

No traveler to any of the countries of the Mediterranean can fail to be impressed by the glorious fruit and vegetable markets with their piles of huge, plump ripe tomatoes, glossy eggplants, colorful bell peppers, giant melons, firm sun-ripened Spanish onions, bunches of fresh herbs and the long braids of Provence garlic...

With such colorful variety, the Mediterraneans have become experts at creating unusual combinations of salads, vegetables, fruits and nuts, sometimes with cheeses or small amounts of fish or meat.

The main-course salad recipes in this section are partly traditional, like the classic Salade Niçoise from France, and partly created by me using typical Mediterranean ingredients readily available here. Most of these dishes also make good first courses, serving about 8 people.

My side salads are ideal accompaniments to plain grilled meat or fish or cheese, and may also be eaten as light appetizers. Some Mediterranean side salads are so simple that they need no recipe: Sliced cucumber with lemon juice and black pepper is wonderful with an oily fish dish; a plate of thickly sliced ripe tomatoes drizzled with oil is marvelous with grilled chicken; cold grilled and sliced red bell peppers or cold cooked fava beans and finely chopped parsley are delicious served with roasted or grilled pork and lamb.

Plainly cooked vegetables are usually the best garnish for main-course dishes. They may be steamed, baked, braised, lightly boiled in a little water, or roasted, and perhaps topped with some chopped fresh herbs such as chives, mint or marjoram. However, if you are serving a plain fish, poultry or meat dish, then it is appropriate to serve a slightly more elaborate vegetable dish. Some of the vegetable recipes here are substantial enough to make satisfying supper dishes on their own, perhaps with the addition of a little grated Parmesan cheese or a chunk of crusty bread.

OPPOSITE: Salade Niçoise (page 106)

MAIN COURSE SALADS

FAVA BEAN & PASTA SALAD IN ORANGE SAUCE
——— *Italy* ———

Calories per serving: 227
Saturated fat: Low
Protein: Medium
Carbohydrate: High
Fiber: 6 g
Cholesterol: 1 mg
Vitamins: C, Niacin, Folic acid
Minerals: Iron, Potassium,
*   Calcium*

5 oz. (dry weight) pasta shells
1-1/4 cups tender fresh young fava
    or lima beans, cooked
2/3 cup canned red kidney beans,
    drained
2/3 cup sliced button mushrooms
1/2 cup *Greek-Style Yogurt* (see
    page 124)
1 orange
1-1/2 tbsp. chopped parsley
Salt and black pepper
8 lettuce leaves
1-1/2 tbsp. chopped walnuts

Cook the pasta shells in boiling salted water until just *al dente*. Drain and let cool slightly, then mix with the beans and mushrooms.

Blend the yogurt with the juice of half of the orange, the parsley and seasoning. Peel and chop the remaining orange and add to the salad. Pour on the dressing, tossing lightly.

Arrange the lettuce in a serving bowl; pile the salad into the center. Scatter the walnuts on the top.

PASTA CRUNCH
——— *Italy* ———

Calories per serving: 390
Saturated fat: Low
Protein: Medium
Carbohydrate: Medium
Fiber: 5 g
Cholesterol: 30 mg
Vitamins: Beta-carotene, C, E,
Niacin, Folic acid
Minerals: Iron, Potassium,
Calcium

6 oz. (dry weight) penne or pasta
    spirals
1 garlic clove, minced
1/4 cup *Oil & Vinegar Dressing* (see
    page 110)
6 oz. cooked chicken meat,
    chopped into small pieces
    (about 3/4 cup)
1 large green bell pepper, seeded
    and chopped
6 oz. broccoli florets, cooked until
    crisp-tender
1 red apple, cored and
    chopped
1/4 cup golden raisins
3 tbsp. pine nuts

Cook the pasta in lightly salted boiling water until just *al dente*. Drain and let cool slightly.

Stir the garlic into the dressing. Combine all the ingredients and serve.

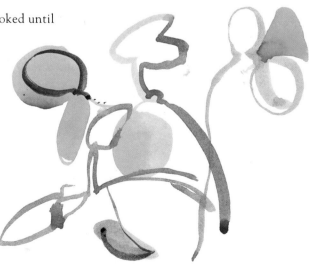

LENTIL & TOMATO SALAD
—— *Italy* ——

Calories per serving: 358
Saturated fat: Low
Protein: Medium
Carbohydrate: Low
Fiber: 8 g
Cholesterol: 62 mg
Vitamins: C, Beta-carotene, D, E
Minerals: Iron, Potassium

1 cup green or brown lentils
1 small onion, halved
1 bay leaf
1 large ripe tomato, chopped
8 green onions, chopped
1/2 cup *Oil & Vinegar Dressing* (see page 110)
1 hard-cooked egg, chopped
3 tbsp. chopped parsley

Cover the lentils with water in a saucepan, add the small onion and bay leaf and simmer until tender—about 1 hour. Drain them, discard the onion and bay leaf, and let them cool slightly.

In a serving dish, combine the lentils with the tomato, green onions and dressing. Sprinkle with the egg and parsley.

AVOCADO WITH MÂCHE
—— *France* ——

Calories per serving: 253
Saturated fat: Medium
Protein: Low
Carbohydrate: Low
Fiber: 3.5 g
Cholesterol: Nil
Vitamins: Beta-carotene, C, Folic acid
Minerals: Potassium, Iron

2 ripe avocados
5 oz. mâche (lamb's lettuce leaves)
8 sprigs of watercress
1 large ripe tomato, seeded and sliced
1 small onion, finely chopped
12 fresh basil leaves, chopped
For the dressing:
3 tbsp. olive oil
1-1/2 tbsp. lemon juice
1 tsp. Dijon-style mustard
1/2 tsp. sugar
Salt and black pepper

Thoroughly combine the dressing ingredients in a small bowl.

Peel, halve, pit and slice the avocados into a bowl. Pour on the dressing to prevent them from discoloring.

Arrange the mâche, watercress, tomato and onion in a serving bowl and add the avocado with the remaining dressing. Garnish with basil leaves.

SEAFOOD SALAD WITH CITRUS DRESSING
—— *Spain* ——

Calories per serving: 238
Saturated fat: Low
Protein: High
Carbohydrate: Low
Fiber: 0.5 g
Cholesterol: 100 mg
Vitamins: C, Beta-carotene
Minerals: Iron, Calcium

3/4 cup white wine
Juice of 1/2 lemon
1/2 lb. prepared squid, sliced
8 chicory leaves
1 (12-oz.) jar mussels in brine, gently rinsed and drained
2-inch piece of cucumber, chopped
1 small red bell pepper, seeded and cut into squares
1-1/2 tbsp. chopped parsley
For the dressing:
1/4 cup olive oil
1-1/2 tbsp. each orange, lemon and lime juice
Salt and black pepper

Put the wine and lemon juice in a small pan with 1 cup of water and bring to a boil. Add the squid and simmer gently 5 minutes, then drain immediately.

Arrange the chicory leaves on a serving plate. Combine the dressing ingredients well. Mix the rest of ingredients with the dressing and pile this on the chicory leaves.

Garnish with orange, lime and lemon slices if desired.

SALADE NIÇOISE
France

Some versions of Salade Niçoise add cooked potatoes, but I prefer to omit them and instead serve the salad with some crusty French bread.

Calories per serving: 328
Saturated fat: Medium
Protein: High
Carbohydrate: Low
Fiber: 3 g
Cholesterol: 291 mg
Vitamins: C, Beta-carotene, E, D, A
Minerals: Iron, Potassium

1 head of Boston or Bibb lettuce
1 large ripe tomato, chopped
3 oz. cooked green beans
6 green onions, halved
1 garlic clove, minced
1/3 cup *Oil & Vinegar Dressing* (see page 110)
2 (7-oz.) cans tuna in oil, drained
6 canned anchovy fillets, drained
8 pitted ripe olives
4 hard-cooked eggs

Remove the outer leaves of the lettuce and tear them into 2 or 3 pieces. Quarter the lettuce heart.

In a serving bowl, combine the torn lettuce and lettuce quarters with the tomato, beans and green onions. Mix the garlic into the dressing and pour half of it into the contents of the bowl. Add the tuna in large chunks and place the anchovy fillets and olives on top.

Pour on the rest of the dressing. Quarter the eggs and arrange them on the top of the salad to serve.

SHRIMP SALAD
Spain

The success of this dish depends upon the avocados being creamy-soft – almost on the point of being over-ripe.

Calories per serving: 526
Saturated fat: Low
Protein: Medium
Carbohydrate: Low
Fiber: 3.5 g
Cholesterol: 162 mg
Vitamins: C, Beta-carotene, E, Folic acid
Minerals: Potassium, Calcium

1-1/3 cups long-grain rice
Large pinch of saffron
1 large or 2 small ripe avocados
1-1/2 tbsp. lemon juice
3/4 lb. peeled cooked shrimp
6 green onions, chopped
1 small green bell pepper, seeded and chopped
1 small red bell pepper, seeded and chopped
1/3 cup *Oil & Vinegar Dressing* (see page 110)

Cook the rice with the saffron in lightly salted boiling water until tender.

Meanwhile, peel, pit and slice the avocado into a bowl with the lemon juice, making sure it is well covered with the juice to prevent discoloration.

When the rice is cooked, drain it and while still warm, combine it in a serving bowl with the rest of the ingredients.

This dish looks good garnished with a few shrimp in their shells. Chopped dill can also be added as a garnish.

OPPOSITE: Shrimp Salad

THREE-NUT SALAD WITH APRICOTS & RAISINS
—————— Italy ——————

This sophisticated salad can also serve 8 as a dinner-party appetizer.

Calories per serving: 306
Saturated fat: Low
Protein: Low
Carbohydrate: Low
Fiber: 7 g
Cholesterol: Nil
Vitamins: E, Beta-carotene, C
Minerals: Iron, Calcium, Potassium

1 small head of radicchio
1 head of Belgian endive
1 bunch of watercress, stems removed
1/2 cup quartered walnuts
1/3 cup almonds
1/3 cup pine nuts
3 tbsp. raisins
3 tbsp. chopped dried apricots
1 celery stalk, chopped
For the dressing:
3 tbsp. walnut or safflower oil
3 tbsp. lemon juice
1/2 tsp. honey
Salt and black pepper

Tear each of the radicchio leaves into 2 or 3 pieces and put them in a serving bowl. Slice the endive into rounds about 1 inch thick and break up a few of them. Add to the bowl with the rest of ingredients.

Combine the dressing ingredients thoroughly and pour onto the salad. Toss well before serving.

MIXED MEDITERRANEAN PLATTER
—————— Italy ——————

The essence of this salad is the variety of lovely colors on one large plate.

Calories per serving: 322
Saturated fat: Medium
Protein: Medium
Carbohydrate: Low
Fiber: 11 g
Cholesterol: 14 mg
Vitamins: Beta-carotene, C, E, Folic acid, Niacin
Minerals: Iron, Calcium

8 radicchio leaves
Young spinach leaves
2/3 cup canned cannellini beans, rinsed and drained
1/4 cup *Oil & Vinegar Dressing* (see page 110)
A few fresh basil leaves, chopped
2-inch piece of cucumber, thinly sliced
12 ears of canned baby corn, drained
2 canned pimientos, drained and sliced
8 pitted ripe olives
1 large ripe tomato, cut into 8 slices
3-1/2 oz. Mozzarella cheese, cut into 8 slices
8 small round slices of whole-wheat bread, about 3 inches diameter, toasted

On a large oval serving platter, arrange the radicchio on one half and the spinach on the other. Toss the beans lightly in 1 tablespoon of the dressing, place them on the radicchio, and garnish with some of the basil.

Arrange the cucumber next to the beans. Place the corn on the spinach and drizzle with a little dressing. Combine the pimiento slices with a little more basil and the olives and arrange this on the spinach.

Place a slice of tomato and then a slice of cheese on each of the bread rounds and broil until the cheese begins to bubble. Don't overcook or the cheese will be dry and leathery.

Arrange the toast in the center of the platter and drizzle any remaining dressing all over the dish.

SIDE SALADS

TOMATO SALAD
———— *France* ————

Calories per serving: 46
Saturated fat: Low
Protein: Low
Carbohydrate: Low
Fiber: 1.5 g
Cholesterol: Nil
Vitamins: Beta-carotene, C, E
Minerals: Potassium

2 large ripe tomatoes, sliced
1-1/2 tbsp. olive oil
Coarse sea salt and black pepper
1 garlic clove, chopped
A few fresh basil leaves, chopped

Arrange the tomato slices on 4 plates. Drizzle with the olive oil. Sprinkle on a little salt and plenty of black pepper and scatter the garlic and basil on top.

CARROT, APPLE & BEET SALAD
———— *Spain* ————

Calories per serving: 97
Saturated fat: Low
Protein: Low
Carbohydrate: Low
Fiber: 2.5 g
Cholesterol: Nil
Vitamins: Beta-carotene, C,
*   Folic acid*
Minerals: Potassium

2 carrots, shredded
1 cooked beet, weighing about
    4 oz., shredded
3 tbsp. raisins
3 tbsp. *Oil & Vinegar Dressing* (see
    page 110)
1 apple

Combine the carrot, beet, raisins and dressing in a serving bowl. Chop the unpeeled apple very finely and add it to the salad.

CELERY & ARTICHOKE SALAD
———— *Italy* ————

I find canned artichoke hearts perfectly acceptable in this dish.

Calories per serving: 108
Saturated fat: Low
Protein: Low
Carbohydrate: Low
Fiber: 3 g
Cholesterol: Nil
Vitamins: Beta-carotene, C
Minerals: Calcium, Potassium

1 heart of celery, cut into
    3-inch strips
1 (14-oz.) can artichoke hearts,
    thoroughly drained and cut into
    halves
8 pitted ripe olives, chopped
1/4 cup *Oil & Vinegar Dressing* (see
    page 110)
A few celery leaves
1 tsp. celery seeds

Arrange the celery and artichoke hearts on salad plates. Divide the olives among the plates.

   Pour some dressing on each plate and garnish with the celery leaves and seeds.

OIL & VINEGAR DRESSING
——— *France* ———

Makes 14 tablespoons
Calories per tbsp: 98
Saturated fat: Low
Protein: Low
Carbohydrate: Low
Fiber: Nil
Cholesterol: Nil
Vitamins: Trace
Minerals: Trace

3/4 cup extra-virgin olive oil
1/4 cup red wine vinegar
1 tsp. mustard powder
1 tsp. sugar
Salt and plenty of black pepper

Combine all the ingredients in a jar with a tight-fitting lid. The dressing will keep for weeks in the refrigerator.

Variations: Add chopped fresh herbs, such as tarragon, oregano or thyme; add minced garlic; use white wine vinegar instead of red.

GREEN SALAD
——— *France* ———

Calories per serving: 56
Saturated fat: Low
Protein: Low
Carbohydrate: Low
Fiber: 1 g
Cholesterol: Nil
Vitamins: Beta-carotene, C, E
Minerals: Iron, Calcium

1/2 head of romaine lettuce
8 chicory leaves
1 bunch of watercress
8 dandelion leaves
3 tbsp. *Oil & Vinegar Dressing* (see above)
Chopped fresh chives, for garnish

Rinse all the leaves in cold water; dry. Tear the romaine leaves and the chicory and chop off most of the watercress stems. Combine all the leaves in a serving bowl with the dressing. Garnish with a few chopped chives.

Variation: For a spicier taste, add a little Belgian endive and/or arugula and radicchio; if you can't find dandelion leaves, use mâche (lamb's lettuce) or oak leaf or butterhead lettuce leaves; for a milder taste, use iceberg lettuce instead of romaine; add some chopped fresh herbs of your choice, such as chervil, basil, parsley or cilantro.

POTATO SALAD
——— *France* ———

Potatoes in salads are often dressed in mayonnaise, but I am sure you will find this version superior.

Calories per serving: 190
Saturated fat: Low
Protein: Low
Carbohydrate: Medium
Fiber: 1.5 g
Cholesterol: Nil
Vitamins: C
Minerals: Potassium

1 lb. new potatoes, scrubbed
1/4 cup *Oil & Vinegar Dressing* (see above)
3 tbsp. chopped fresh mint
3 tbsp. chopped parsley
4 large green onions, chopped

Cook the potatoes in boiling salted water until just tender, then drain and chop them roughly into a serving bowl. While the potatoes are still warm, add all the other ingredients and mix lightly. Cover and let stand about 1 hour before serving.

OPPOSITE: Green Salad with Oil & Vinegar Dressing; Potato Salad

TABBOULEH
—— *Lebanon* ——

Tabbouleh can be served as an appetizer. It also goes well with grilled lamb and fish.

Calories per serving: 170
Saturated fat: Low
Protein: Low
Carbohydrate: Medium
Fiber: 4 g
Cholesterol: Nil
Vitamins: Beta-carotene, C, E
Minerals: Calcium, Iron, Potassium

3/4 cup bulgur wheat
1 head of romaine lettuce
1 large ripe tomato, seeded and chopped
8 green onions, chopped
3-inch piece of cucumber, chopped
1 bunch of fresh mint, chopped
1 bunch of parsley, chopped
3 tbsp. olive oil
3 tbsp. lemon juice
Salt and black pepper

Cover the bulgur with water and let it swell about 20 minutes. Drain well. Arrange the lettuce leaves around the edge of 4 serving dishes. Combine all the remaining ingredients with the bulgur and pile on the serving dishes.

ORANGE & FENNEL SALAD
—— *Italy* ——

This salad goes particularly well with oily fish and pork.

Calories per serving: 160
Saturated fat: Low
Protein: Low
Carbohydrate: Low
Fiber: 5 g
Cholesterol: Nil
Vitamins: C, Niacin, Beta-carotene
Minerals: Potassium, Calcium, Iron

1 large or 2 small fennel bulbs
2 large or 3 small oranges
1/3 cup olive oil
1-1/2 tbsp. lemon juice
Salt and black pepper
1/3 cup chopped parsley or cilantro leaves
A few anise seeds

Core and slice the fennel, keeping a few leaves to garnish the salad. Segment or thinly slice the oranges and arrange them on serving plates with the fennel slices in the center.

Blend the olive oil, lemon juice and seasoning and drizzle this on the salads. Sprinkle the chopped parsley or cilantro leaves and the anise seeds on top and garnish with fennel leaves.

BEAN SALAD
—— *Italy* ——

Calories per serving: 192
Saturated fat: Low
Protein: Medium
Carbohydrate: Low
Fiber: 11 g
Cholesterol: Nil
Vitamins: C
Minerals: Potassium, Calcium

1 cup dried navy beans, soaked in water overnight
1 bay leaf
1/4 cup *Oil & Vinegar Dressing* (see page 110)
1 garlic clove, minced
2 celery stalks, chopped
4 green onions, chopped
1-1/2 tbsp. chopped parsley

Drain the beans. Put them in a saucepan with water to cover and boil 10 minutes, then turn the heat down, add the bay leaf and simmer gently until tender–up to 2 hours. Drain and mix with the rest of the ingredients while still warm.

OPPOSITE: Orange & Fennel Salad; Tabbouleh

VEGETABLES

PURÉED PUMPKIN
———— *France* ————

Calories per serving: 100
Saturated fat: Low
Protein: Low
Carbohydrate: Low
Fiber: 1.5 g
Cholesterol: Nil
Vitamins: Beta-carotene, C
Minerals: Potassium

1-1/2-lb. piece of pumpkin, peeled, seeded and cubed
Pinch of sugar
2 garlic cloves, chopped
2 tbsp. olive oil
Salt
1 tsp. paprika
1 tbsp. toasted sesame seeds

Preheat the oven to 350F (175C).

In a shallow ovenproof dish mix the pumpkin with the rest of the ingredients except the seeds. Cover and bake 30 minutes to 1 hour, until tender.

Let cool slightly, then purée in a blender. Sprinkle with the sesame seeds before serving.

Variation: You can use this recipe for sweet potatoes, but the calorie count will go up to 205.

PURÉED POTATOES
———— *France* ————

Most people add butter to puréed potatoes, but this recipe is a healthier alternative.

Calories per serving: 197
Saturated fat: Low
Protein: Low
Carbohydrate: High
Fiber: 2 g
Cholesterol: Nil
Vitamins: C
Minerals: Potassium

1-1/2 lb. russet potatoes
3 tbsp. olive oil
Salt and pepper
3 tbsp. *Greek-Style Yogurt* (see page 124)

Cook the potatoes in their skins in boiling salted water. Peel them and chop them into a bowl. Add the olive oil, salt and pepper and mash to a purée. Fold in the yogurt just before serving.

RATATOUILLE
———— *France* ————

Some versions of ratatouille contain little eggplant, but I prefer it to be dominant.

Calories per serving: 143
Saturated fat: Low
Protein: Low
Carbohydrate: Low
Fiber: 5.5 g
Cholesterol: Nil
Vitamins: Beta-carotene, C, E
Minerals: Potassium, Iron

1 large eggplant
2 zucchini
1/4 cup olive oil
1 large onion, sliced
1 large garlic clove, chopped
1 green bell pepper, seeded and sliced
Salt and black pepper
1 cup canned tomatoes
2 tbsp. chopped fresh basil or 2 tsp. dried basil

Slice the eggplant and zucchini, sprinkle them with salt and let them drain in a colander about 30 minutes. Rinse and pat the pieces dry.

Heat the oil in a Dutch oven over medium heat and sauté the onion until soft. Add the garlic and sauté 1 minute more. Add the eggplant, zucchini, bell pepper and seasoning. Cover and simmer 40 minutes. Then add the tomatoes and basil and simmer, uncovered, 20 minutes longer.

SPINACH WITH GARLIC & OIL
—————— Italy ——————

Calories per serving: 95
Saturated fat: Low
Protein: High
Carbohydrate: Low
Fiber: 10 g
Cholesterol: Nil
Vitamins: Beta-carotene, C, E
Minerals: Potassium, Calcium

1-1/2 lb. fresh spinach, rinsed and
   chopped
1-1/2 tbsp. olive oil
1 garlic clove, chopped
Pinch of grated nutmeg
Salt and black pepper
3 tbsp. grated Parmesan cheese

Cook the spinach in the water clinging to its leaves in a covered saucepan until wilted. Drain.

Heat the oil in a skillet over medium heat and stir-fry the spinach with the garlic and nutmeg 1–2 minutes. Season to taste, transfer to a serving dish, and top with the cheese.

SWISS CHARD WITH PINE NUTS
—————— Italy ——————

Calories per serving: 80
Saturated fat: Low
Protein: High
Carbohydrate: Low
Fiber: 6.5 g
Cholesterol: Nil
Vitamins: Beta-carotene, C, E
Minerals: Iron, Calcium

1 lb. Swiss chard leaves, trimmed
1-1/2 tbsp. olive oil
3 tbsp. pine nuts
2 garlic cloves, chopped
Pinch of grated nutmeg
Salt and black pepper

Parboil the chard for a few minutes; drain.

Heat the oil in a skillet over medium heat and sauté the pine nuts until golden. Remove with a slotted spoon. Sauté the chard about 2 minutes, adding the garlic for the last minute.

Season with nutmeg, salt and pepper. Scatter on the pine nuts and serve.

GREEN BEANS IN ORANGE SAUCE
—————— France ——————

Calories per serving: 75
Saturated fat: Low
Protein: Low
Carbohydrate: Low
Fiber: 3.5 g
Cholesterol: Nil
Vitamins: C, E
Minerals: Potassium

1 lb. young green beans
1-1/2 tbsp. olive oil
2 green onions, finely chopped
1 tsp. Dijon style-mustard
1-1/2 tbsp. orange juice
Dash of white wine vinegar

Trim the beans and parboil them in lightly salted water 2 minutes; drain.

Heat the oil in a skillet over medium heat, add the onions and stir-fry 1 minute. Add the mustard, orange juice and vinegar and stir-fry 1 minute more. Add the beans, stir-fry 1 minute, then serve.

BELL PEPPER & TOMATO STEW
—————— Spain ——————

Calories per serving: 66
Saturated fat: Low
Protein: Low
Carbohydrate: Low
Fiber: 3 g
Cholesterol: Nil
Vitamins: Beta-carotene, C, E
Minerals: Potassium

1 green bell pepper
1-1/2 tbsp. olive oil
1 onion, thinly sliced
1 garlic clove, chopped
2 large ripe tomatoes, sliced
1 tsp. ground coriander
1 tsp. ground cumin
Salt and black pepper

Seed and slice the bell pepper.

Heat the oil in a heavy saucepan over medium heat and sauté the onion until soft. Add the garlic and bell pepper and sauté 1 minute. Add the rest of the ingredients, cover and simmer, 30 minutes.

Variation: Omit the spices and add 2 tablespoons of chopped fresh basil.

OVERLEAF: Puréed Pumpkin; Swiss Chard with Pine Nuts

BREAKFASTS
& DESSERTS

Even a diet of the healthiest lunches and suppers can be sabotaged if you continue to indulge in heavy fried breakfasts and sugary desserts.

Here instead are some light and healthy Mediterranean-style carbohydrate-rich breakfast choices and mouth-watering desserts based on fruit.

The North American passion for animal protein at breakfast time–slices of bacon, sausages, eggs, ham, and so on–is virtually non-existent among the peoples of the Mediterranean region.

Breakfast in Spain, Italy, Greece and the South of France is much more of a high-carbohydrate affair. Carbohydrate is, in fact, a much more sensible breakfast, as it is more quickly converted by the body into much-needed energy to get you started for the day.

The perfect breakfast is plenty of fresh crusty bread with preserves or honey, some fresh fruit juice or fruit and–for the big breakfast eater–some Greek-style yogurt.

The yogurt of the Eastern Mediterranean is strained and beautifully thick and creamy. It may seem like a real indulgence until you discover that it has, in fact, less fat than half-and-half.

However, for calorie-watchers, I have devised an even lower-fat, lower-calorie version, which tastes almost as good as the real thing and is easy to make. If you prefer to buy real Greek yogurt, be aware that it contains 20 calories per tablespoon rather than the 10 in my version. Ordinary low-fat plain yogurt can also be used in most of the recipes and at breakfast; some brands taste creamier and richer than others.

Desserts in the Mediterranean were traditionally fairly simple and usually based on fruit. It is only recently in the more affluent areas, and with the increase in tourism, that desserts in restaurants in the area have become elaborate, more fat-laden and less healthy.

I would almost always choose to end any Mediterranean meal with fresh fruit, but I have included a few more elaborate dessert recipes as everyone enjoys an indulgence now and then–and I am no exception in this!

OPPOSITE: Peaches in Wine (page 120)

MIXED FRUIT COMPOTE
———— Tunisia ————

Calories per serving: 260
Saturated fat: Nil
Protein: Low
Carbohydrate: High
Fiber: 18 g
Cholesterol: Nil
Vitamins: A, C, Beta-carotene
Minerals: Iron, Potassium

6 oz. dried apricots or peaches
4 oz. pitted prunes
2 cups orange juice
2 oranges
2 bananas
6 tbsp. raisins

In an ovenproof dish soak the apricots and prunes overnight in the orange juice.

Preheat the oven to 350F (175C).

Peel and slice the oranges and bananas into rounds and add them and the raisins to the dish. Bake 30 minutes, and serve hot or cold.

Variations: You can vary the fruit according to what is available; try figs or dates instead of prunes.

PEACHES IN WINE
———— France ————

Calories per serving: 115
Saturated fat: Nil
Protein: Low
Carbohydrate: High
Fiber: 1.5 g
Cholesterol: Nil
Vitamins: C, Beta-carotene
Minerals: Potassium

4 ripe peaches
2 tbsp. sugar
Juice of 1/2 lemon
About 1 cup dessert wine, such as a Muscat

Peel the peaches and slice them into serving dishes. Sprinkle with the sugar and lemon juice.

Before serving, add enough wine just to cover the peaches.

CITRUS & HONEY DESSERT
———— Italy ————

Calories per serving: 140
Saturated fat: Low
Protein: Low
Carbohydrate: Medium
Fiber: 3 g
Cholesterol: Nil
Vitamins: C, E, Beta-carotene
Minerals: Potassium

2 oranges
2 ruby grapefruit
Juice of 1/2 lemon
1/4 cup orange juice
3 tbsp. honey
3 tbsp. chopped mixed nuts, for garnish

Peel and section the oranges and grapefruit and arrange them in serving bowls.

Stir together the juices and honey and heat gently in a small pan, or in the microwave oven. Pour onto the fruit, and garnish with the chopped nuts.

APPLE & DATE COMPOTE
—— *Greece* ——

Calories per serving: 155
Saturated fat: Low
Protein: Low
Carbohydrate: High
Fiber: 6 g
Cholesterol: Nil
Vitamins: C, Folic acid
Minerals: Potassium

4 large apples
1/3 cup chopped dates
1/2 tsp. ground cinnamon
Juice of 2 oranges
3 tbsp. honey
3 tbsp. sesame seeds

Preheat the oven to 375F (190C).

Peel and slice the apples into a shallow ovenproof dish and mix in the dates with the cinnamon. Pour on the orange juice and honey and top with the sesame seeds. Bake 30 minutes.

BANANA & STRAWBERRY SORBETS
—— *Italy* ——

Calories per serving: 185
Saturated fat: Low
Protein: Low
Carbohydrate: High
Fiber: 3 g
Cholesterol: Trace
Vitamins: Beta-carotene, C
Minerals: Iron, Potassium

1/2 cup sugar
2 ripe bananas
3 tbsp. lemon juice
3/4 cup *Greek-Style Yogurt* (see page 124)
1-1/2 cups ripe strawberries
Strawberry leaves, for garnish

Dissolve the sugar in 1 cup water and boil to make a syrup. Mash the bananas with half of the lemon juice, the yogurt, and half of the syrup.

Purée the strawberries with the rest of the lemon juice and syrup. Still-freeze both mixtures in separate containers, removing from the freezer from time to time to whisk.

Serve a spoonful of each sorbet to each person, garnished with the strawberry leaves.

Variations: Use raspberries instead of strawberries, or melon or mango instead of one of the bananas.

MELON & STRAWBERRY SALAD
—— *Italy* ——

Calories per serving: 80
Saturated fat: Nil
Protein: Low
Carbohydrate: High
Fiber: 3.5 g
Cholesterol: Nil
Vitamins: Beta-carotene, C, Folic acid
Minerals: Iron

2 small ripe cantaloupe melons
1 pint ripe strawberries
1-1/2 tbsp. lemon juice
1 tbsp. sugar
12 fresh mint leaves

Halve the melons horizontally, remove and discard the seeds, and scoop out the flesh, reserving the shells. Hull the strawberries and coarsely chop them. Sprinkle with the lemon juice and sugar and macerate 30 minutes.

Mix the melon flesh and strawberries and pile this back into the melon shells. Decorate with the mint leaves.

OVERLEAF: Mixed Fruit Compote; Citrus & Honey Dessert; Apple & Date Compote

BAKED PEARS
France

Calories per serving: 172
Saturated fat: Nil
Protein: Low
Carbohydrate: High
Fiber: 3 g
Cholesterol: Nil
Vitamins: C
Minerals: Potassium

4 firm pears
1/2 cup sugar
1/2 bottle of red wine
1 cinnamon stick
4 whole cloves

Preheat the oven to 325F (170C).

Peel the pears, leaving the stems on. Place them in an ovenproof dish with the sugar and wine. Add the cinnamon stick and the cloves and enough water to cover.

Bake about 40 minutes or until the pears are tender. If the juice is too thin, reduce it in a saucepan. Pour it over the pears and serve cold.

Variations: Pears can also be cooked this way in a covered saucepan over a very low heat.

GREEK-STYLE YOGURT
Greece

The secret of making good yogurt lies in using a good fresh starter. Also keep all your utensils sterilized and do not leave the yogurt longer than necessary to set.

Calories per 1/2 cup serving: 67
Saturated fat: Low
Protein: High
Carbohydrate: Medium
Fiber: Nil
Cholesterol: 4.5 mg
Vitamins: Niacin, A
Minerals: Calcium

2 tbsp. nonfat dry milk powder
2-1/4 cups skim milk
2 tbsp. plain yogurt with live culture

Dissolve the milk powder in the milk and simmer 5 minutes. Pour into a heatproof bowl and let cool until you can just dip a finger in it. Add the yogurt and stir. Cover the bowl with plastic wrap, wrap it in a thick towel, and leave it in a warm place 5–6 hours. Alternatively, you can make the yogurt in a wide-necked vacuum bottle.

When it is set, pour off the thin whey on top and pass the yogurt through a strainer lined with layers of paper towels, set over a bowl. Leave 30 minutes by which time the yogurt will have thickened. Put in a covered container and refrigerate. Use 2 tablespoons of this yogurt to start your next batch.

OPPOSITE: Greek-Style Yogurt with fresh fruit

INDEX

INDEX

HEIGHT/WEIGHT CHART FOR WOMEN

Height	Average weight	Acceptable weight range
4 ft 11 in	104 lb	94–122 lb
5 ft 0 in	107 lb	96–125 lb
5 ft 1in	110 lb	99–128 lb
5 ft 2 in	113 lb	102–131 lb
5 ft 3 in	116 lb	105–134 lb
5 ft 4 in	120 lb	108–138 lb
5 ft 5 in	123 lb	111–142 lb
5 ft 6 in	128 lb	114–146 lb
5 ft 7 in	132 lb	118–150 lb
5 ft 8 in	136 lb	122–154 lb
5 ft 9 in	140 lb	126–158 lb
5 ft 10 in	144 lb	130–163 lb
5 ft 11 in	148 lb	134–168 lb

HEIGHT/WEIGHT CHART FOR MEN

Height	Average weight	Acceptable weight range
5 ft 4 in	130 lb	118–148 lb
5 ft 5 in	133 lb	121–152 lb
5 ft 6in	136 lb	124–156 lb
5 ft 7 in	140 lb	128–161 lb
5 ft 8 in	145 lb	132–166 lb
5 ft 9 in	149 lb	136–170 lb
5 ft 10 in	153 lb	140–174 lb
5 ft 11 in	158 lb	144–179 lb
6 ft 0 in	162 lb	148–184 lb
6 ft 1 in	166 lb	152–189 lb
6 ft 2 in	171 lb	156–194 lb
6 ft 3 in	176 lb	160–199 lb
6 ft 4 in	181 lb	164–204 lb